A Life of Solid Principles

SUNY series in Contemporary Continental Philosophy

Dennis J. Schmidt, editor

A Life of Solid Principles

The Philosopher of Extremes

Edgar Bauer

Translated, with a Preface and Afterword by

Charles Barbour

SUNY PRESS

Published by State University of New York Press, Albany

Links to third-party websites are provided as a convenience and for informational purposes only. They do not constitute an endorsement or an approval of any of the products, services, or opinions of the organization, companies, or individuals. SUNY Press bears no responsibility for the accuracy, legality, or content of a URL, the external website, or for that of subsequent websites.

EU GPSR Authorised Representative:
Logos Europe, 9 rue Nicolas Poussin, 17000, La Rochelle, France
contact@logoseurope.eu
For information, contact State University of New York Press, Albany, NY
www.sunypress.edu

Library of Congress Cataloging-in-Publication Data

Names: Bauer, Edgar, author | Barbour, Charles, editor
Title: A life of solid principles: The philosopher of extremes / Edgar Bauer, author, and Charles Barbour, editor.
Description: Albany : State University of New York Press, [2025] | Includes bibliographical references and index.
Identifiers: ISBN 9798855804393 (hardcover) | ISBN 9798855804416 (ebook) | ISBN 9798855804409 (paperback)

Further information is available at the Library of Congress.

Contents

Biographical Note

Edgar Bauer was born in 1820, in the town of Charlottenburg near Berlin. Initially intending to follow in his older brother Bruno Bauer's footsteps, he began to study theology at the University of Berlin just as Bruno started to come into conflict with church and state authorities. He experienced a loss of faith and, in 1841, abandoned his university career to become a writer. He wrote dozens of articles and reviews for the radical press that was taking shape around the Young Hegelians (including the *Deutsche Jahrbücher* and the *Rheinische Zeitung*) as well as longer monographs and pamphlets on political theory, political history, and contemporary political events. When, in 1843, he sought to publish his *Der Streit der Kritik mit Kirche und Staat* in Prussia without governmental approval, all copies were confiscated by the police, and he was subjected to a lengthy legal proceeding at the end of which he was found guilty of insulting religious society, mocking the law, and arousing dissatisfaction with the state. In 1845 he began serving an eight-year sentence at Magdeburg Prison. But he was released at the outbreak of the 1848 Revolutions, during which he agitated for radical democracy. As the revolutions began to fail in 1849, he fled first to Hanover and then to Altona, where he became involved in the Schleswig-Holstein independence movement. In 1851, however, he appears to have changed sides. With the support of the Danish government, he emigrated to London, where he continued to work as a journalist. From 1852 to 1861, he was paid by the Danish police to write secret reports on the activities of European exiles living in London. After the Prussian King Wilhelm I issued his 1861 amnesty for 1848 revolutionaries, Bauer returned to Germany where he became founding editor of the conservative *Kirchliche Blatter*. However, his support for the Hanover separatist Guelph Party left him once again out of favor with Prussian authorities and curtailed his opportunities as a journalist. Destitute and largely forgotten, he died in Hanover in 1886.

Preface

In the spring of 1843, the Young Hegelian movement was in disarray. Not long before, the group had occupied a commanding position in German literary culture, from which they boldly and notoriously attacked the established political and religious order. By early 1843, however, they found themselves on the receiving end of a swift and aggressive reaction organized by conservative elements within the regime of the Prussian King Friedrich Wilhelm IV. Key figures in the movement had already been excluded or purged from the universities and other positions of power within the Prussian state. Now their journals were being suppressed, and their books were being banned. Worse still, a newly formed Ober Censurgericht or Higher Censorship Court threatened to impose even harsher penalties on dissent — penalties that would soon see a number of the most outspoken Young Hegelians arrested, put on trial, and imprisoned for significant amounts of time. Under the pressure, already-existing tensions were exacerbated, and the movement began to splinter. Some, such as Karl Marx and Arnold Ruge, chose to move to Paris and other European cities in self-imposed exile, and to continue the struggle from a safer distance. Others, including the faction organized around the controversial Bible critic Bruno Bauer, decided to stay in Germany and mount a battle against the censorship head-on. At the same time, the political and theological disputes that had characterized Young Hegelianism in its initial manifestation were being supplemented and perhaps even overshadowed by a new concern with the so-called social question, and a new fascination with the socialist and communist theories emerging out of France. Everyone was scrambling to find their bearings on an almost continuously shifting terrain. And everyone was vying to be recognized as the most radical, the most extreme, or the one who had "gone the furthest."[1]

It was in this heady atmosphere that the Young Hegelian who arguably *was* the most radical — Bruno Bauer's younger brother Edgar Bauer — wrote and published an intriguing novella called *Es leben feste Grundsätze!* or *A Life of Solid Principles!* Speaking directly to the multiple crises of its time, it tells the story of an idealistic young man named — significantly enough — Karl, of his political disillusionment, and of his inexorable fall from grace. As the novella opens, we learn that Karl's aging father, the old Herr Geheim-Secretair or Secret Secretary, has spent the final years of his life securing a position for his son in the Prussian civil service. But, swept up by the dynamism of his generation, Karl scandalously refuses the appointment to pursue a career as a writer and a journalist. For this betrayal, Karl's father curses him from his deathbed. But for a long period, and despite many hardships, Karl remains committed to his principles, and thus in a sense untouched by his father's curse. He rails against the arbitrary power of the state and the church, against economic injustice and aristocratic privilege, against hypocritical morality, the unequal treatment of women, and the corrupt institution of marriage, and especially against the censorship. Ultimately, however, and in part because of his doctrinaire disposition, he is left destitute and humiliated, living in poverty with his disgraced sister and her bastard son amid Berlin's urban proletariat. And when Karl's chief antagonist in the novella — the scheming and unscrupulous Baron Arthur — finds out about his situation, he is able to orchestrate one final humiliation: the offer of a lucrative job with the censorship authority. Feeling he has no other choice, the once-proud Karl grovelingly accepts the post, and ends the novella as a state employee charged with the task of monitoring and policing the very radical press for which he once wrote.

Es Leben feste Grundsätze! originally appeared as the second of two novellas in a coauthored volume titled *Berliner Novellen*, where it was preceded by the slightly more famous Alexandre Weill's *Ein Winter in Berlin*. While it received a handful of reviews when it first appeared, *Es Leben feste Grundsätze!* never became the object of scholarly attention, nor is there anything like a history of commentary on the work.[2] It was, for 180 years, more or less forgotten. But the recent past has witnessed a spate of new interest in the Young Hegelians, and in the German Vormärz in general, or the period in German history immediately prior to the 1848 Revolutions. Whereas during the twentieth century the Young Hegelians tended to be seen through the lens of Marx's and Engels's vicious polemics against them in works like *The Holy Family* and the collection of manuscripts known as *The German Ideology*, more recent scholarship has sought to approach these figures on their own terms, and to develop a clearer picture of what they were attempting to accomplish and how they were attempting to do so.[3] We can now say with confidence that they were not the abstract and ineffectual figures Marx and Engels made them out to be, nor were they exclusively concerned with theological problems. On the contrary, they were institutional warriors. And their writings were designed, not to contemplate obtuse philosophical puzzles, but to accomplish specific tasks in specific — and extremely concrete — institutional battles. Moreover, and perhaps more importantly, while their thought is undoubtedly complex and involved, articulated as it often is in the discrete political theological idiom of its time, it nevertheless represents a significant if overlooked moment in the history of radical political theory, and especially the history of revolutionary republicanism. The first and most obvious purpose of the current volume, then, is to contribute to this emerging body of literature, and to do so in at least two ways: first, by providing a translation of *Es Leben feste Grundsätze!* thereby augmenting our knowledge of the literary aspect of Young Hegelianism; and second, by supplementing that translation with an extended interpretive essay on the work and career of its author, Edgar Bauer — a figure who, despite the growth of interest in the Vormärz, remains surprisingly understudied and unknown.[4]

But beyond the new insights that it offers into the intellectual history of the nineteenth century, there are at least two further reasons to revisit *Es leben feste Grundsätze!* today, the first more dramatic, or more likely to pique our immediate interest, but the second, I would suggest, more important. The first is based on a recent article by the Belgian scholar Herbert De Vriese. De Vriese, who is probably the only person to engage seriously with *Es leben feste Grundsätze!* since it appeared, makes the striking claim that the Karl character is at least loosely based on Karl Marx.[5] As De Vriese explains, Edgar Bauer wrote the novella amid an acrimonious dispute within the Young Hegelian movement that pitted the Berlin faction to which he belonged, on the one side, against Karl Marx and Arnold Ruge, on the other. In essence, during the second half of 1842, the Berlin Young Hegelians (a group that also referred to itself as The Free, and that, along with Edgar Bauer, included Eduard Meyen, Ludwig Buhl, Karl Köppen, Karl Nauwreck, and Max Stirner) had begun to pursue a strategy of provoking the authorities by publicly declaring their commitments to atheism and revolution. Marx and Ruge saw this approach as subjectivist and voluntaristic. Its only consequence, they believed, would be the loss of popular support and suppression of the movement. They thus responded by openly renouncing the members of The Free. The effect was particularly glaring in the pages of the *Rheinische Zeitung*, which had previously carried regular articles by Berlin correspondents, but which, after Marx became editor on October 15, 1842, stopped publishing them altogether. On De Vriese's account, Bauer's unflattering portrayal of Karl as someone who, in the end, slavishly abandons his radical principles to become an agent of the government was designed to exact a kind of literary revenge on Marx. It suggested, in other words, that Marx would similarly betray the cause. And its goal was to destroy Marx's reputation among the Young Hegelians.

The evidence De Vriese assembles for his interpretation, if not conclusive, is difficult to ignore. For instance, Karl begins the novella in a relationship with the socially superior Marie, who is the daughter of a privy councillor in the Prussian government. At the time Bauer finished working on *Es Leben feste Grundsätze!* in early 1843, Marx was engaged to the socially superior Jenny von Westphalen, daughter of Ludwig von Westphalen, who was privy councillor to the Prussian government of the Rhine Province. In the novella, Marie's father proudly displays his Fourth-Class Order of the Red Eagle, an honor awarded by the Prussian king to loyal military officers and civil servants. Ludwig von Westphalen also possessed the Fourth-Class Order of the Red Eagle, which had been given to him for loyal service by the Prussian King Friedrich Wilhelm III. Perhaps more specifically, and as noted above, *Es leben feste Grundsätze!* begins with Karl rejecting his father's plan for him to enter the civil service and defiantly taking up a career as a journalist. Indeed, during one of their heated encounters, Arthur even identifies Karl as an employee of the *Rheinische Zeitung*. Karl Marx also quarreled bitterly with his father over his chosen career. And, as is well-known, he was one of the key figures behind the *Rheinische Zeitung*. Less substantively, but still intriguingly, Marie's cousin Gustav, who returns from abroad in the second half of the novella, has certain similarities with Jenny von Westphalen's brother and Marx's lifelong friend Edgar von Westphalen. And, finally, the overall demeanor of the Karl character — deeply opinionated, terrifyingly intelligent, acerbically witty, more than a little arrogant, and easily provoked into an argument — sits well alongside all reports we have of the young Marx's personality, and much of what we find in his personal correspondence. For De Vriese, then, what we might have in *Es leben feste Grundsätze!* is a very rare thing indeed — a fictionalized portrait of one of the most important figures in our entire intellectual tradition, and one that has, until now, remained completely unknown.

All of that said, it would, I think, be possible to push De Vriese's suggestion too far. For while it seems likely that Edgar Bauer had Marx somewhere in mind when creating the Karl character, it would be wrong to think that Marx was the only idealistic young journalist becoming disillusioned or questioning his fundamental principles at the time. In fact, it would be more accurate to say that the entire Young Hegelian movement was living through this experience. For, from the time of its inception (which can probably best be dated to January 1838, when, along with Theodore Echtermeyer, Ruge began to publish the *Hallische Jahrbücher*), the defining characteristic of Young Hegelianism was its commitment to the concept of the state. More precisely, from 1838 to 1843, the Young Hegelians advanced a republican conception of freedom, and held that freedom cannot be understood as mere independence or freedom from external interference but can only be achieved through direct and ongoing participation in public life. And, following but also radicalizing Hegel's *Philosophy of Right*, they believed that the modern state (and only the modern state) could provide the normative and institutional framework for the realization of freedom in this sense.[6] When, in 1842 and 1843, the same modern state that they venerated was turned into a weapon to be used against them (when it did not submit to the claims of reason, as Hegel had suggested it would, but remained a vehicle for religious mystification and arbitrary power), it was not only Marx who became disillusioned with political struggles within the state. It was nearly all the Young Hegelians. Including, perhaps more than any other, Edgar Bauer. Thus, and without a doubt, the Karl in *Es leben feste Grundsätze!* has enticing similarities to Karl Marx. But his experience of a political loss of faith was much more widespread at the time than that suggests. And some elements of it could even be called universal.

This brings us to the second, more substantial reason to revisit *Es leben feste Grundsätze!* today. It is not merely a fictionalised portrait of Marx. It is a serious work of literature in its own right, a sometimes-profound philosophical reflection on the vicissitudes of political change, and a significant piece of social history. It depicts a world in which all established values — all solid principles or firm foundations (*feste Grundsätze*) — are being progressively eroded or exposed as hollow and indefensible. And not only Karl but all the characters are searching desperately for new principles, or new ways of living with both others and themselves. Thus, along with Karl, who struggles with his father over the proper vocation of a young middle-class man, and how such a man should contribute to the political life of the people and the state, we find Marie struggling with both the restrictive gender roles that nineteenth-century society imposes on her and Karl's myopic suggestion that she can simply abandon those roles unscathed, and that she submit to the equally restrictive dictates of what he calls reason. Similarly, we find Karl's sister, little Clare, struggling to understand the nature of love, and to break free from the narrow horizons imposed on her by her father, only to be seduced and mercilessly cast aside by Baron Arthur. But Arthur also struggles to find purpose in a world that increasingly has none for him, and that locates its highest values, not in the aristocratic tradition of honor that had motivated his ancestors, but in bourgeois financial acumen and the accumulation of wealth. Both Marie's cousin Gustav and, perhaps most explicitly, the proletarian shoemaker Albert (who are introduced in the novella's second part, after Arthur has successfully courted Marie and married her for her fortune) are also searching for the new principles that will guide them, the first believing that he will discover them by cultivating a philanthropic attitude toward the poor (an ostensibly noble pursuit that is ultimately revealed to be condescending and self-interested), and the second, after adopting a whole series of "philosophies" as he calls them, coming to the conclusion that he will only discover them in himself.

Because of its light and comedic mood, it is easy, perhaps, to miss the sophisticated literary composition of *Es leben feste Grundsätze!* But it is divided into two parts, and that division formally articulates the central thematic tension between publicity and privacy. Thus, and in good republican fashion, Bauer's narrator spends much of part 1 reminding the reader of the virtues of public life and the corruption and decay of a world without it, or a world in which individuals are confined to the darkness and isolation of the private sphere. The open political discourse of writers and journalists like Karl, for example, is contrasted with the archaic bureaucratic order of secret secretaries and privy councillors. And each of the vices that the main characters fall into — everything from the Herr Geheim-Secretair's patriarchal intransigence to Arthur's vain superficiality to little Clare's naive susceptibility — is attributed to a lack of political community, or a lack of opportunities to participate meaningfully in a human social world. But then, in a manner that intriguingly mirrors the Young Hegelians' loss of faith in politics and the modern state and turn toward the proletariat and the social question, part 2 directs us away from the boulevards, cafés, and theaters of Berlin's city center to the narrow alleys and cramped apartments of its working-class slums, where Karl, little Clare, and little Clare's child are found living with Albert. And we are given to understand that, even if the ideal republican public sphere were to be accomplished, it would still be founded on a material, class-based infrastructure of misery and exploitation. Here the narrator has far fewer easy answers than in the first part of the novella. And in the end, Karl only escapes poverty and participates in the life of the state by betraying his principles, while little Clare and Albert only preserve their principles by remaining isolated, powerless, and poor.

How Bauer handles the setting and the genre of his contribution to the *Berliner Novellen* is equally complex. Both issues are invoked straightaway, in the work's curious opening section, which consists of a paratextual and metafictional letter from the author of the story we are about to read to an unnamed friend. The friend, we discover, has "almost mockingly" challenged the author to compose a "Berlin novella" or "romance," by which he means the popular Romantic melodramas of the time, notably the work of French novelists like Prosper Mérimée, Théophile Gautier, Alfred de Musset, or Eugène Sue. To understand why the author's friend thinks Berlin would be such an unlikely setting for a Romantic narrative of this sort, it is helpful to know that, for the first half of the nineteenth century, Berlin had a reputation for being rather boring and prosaic. Of course, it had long been the seat of government. And it was the center of Prussia's expansive bureaucracy and its powerful military. But it lacked the deep navigable waterways required for large-scale industry and trade. As a result, it was something of a sleepy government town populated primarily by civil servants and career soldiers. That, however, changed rapidly with the introduction of the railway in the early 1840s, or the period when Bauer was working on *Es leben feste Grundsätze!* For the railway transformed Berlin into a hub of economic activity. Almost overnight, the sleepy government town became a modern industrial city — replete with a large, volatile urban proletariat.[7] Like a handful of other works that appeared around the same time — including Ernst Dronke's *Berlin*, Friedrich Sass's *Berlin in seiner neuesten Zeit und Entwicklung*, and the popular multivolume exposé of Berlin's criminal underworld *Die Geheimnisse von Berlin: Aus den Papieren eines Berliner Kriminalbeamten* — Bauer's and Weill's *Berliner Novellen* formed part of a larger effort to give literary expression to this upheaval, and to represent a Berlin that was not dull and obedient, but vibrant, dynamic, and alive.[8]

Along with preparing us for a portrait of the new Berlin, the letter at the beginning of *Es leben feste Grundsätze!* serves another, equally important purpose. For if the author's friend suggests that the city of Berlin is inadequate to the exaggerated melodrama, prurient scandals, and intense emotions of popular novellas and romances, the author's reply suggests that such familiar Romantic tropes are inadequate to the city of Berlin, and to the new social relations being forged in modern urban environments. Here Bauer follows other Young Hegelians (notably Arnold Ruge) in breaking definitively with Romanticism, and thus opening the question of what new literary forms or styles will emerge to capture this new literary content, or what forms will emerge out of this new experience of the city.[9] No doubt the easy answer would be some manifestation of social realism, and elements of *Es leben feste Grundsätze!* certainly point in that direction. And yet, the piece also experiments quite broadly with literary forms, including both third- and first-person narration, multiple and shifting focalizers, epistolary chapters made up of personal correspondence between the characters, and even at the end an entire chapter scripted as a theatrical scene. And this formal experimentation foregrounds the fictional or artificial status of the work. But maybe the most distinctive aspect of *Es leben feste Grundsätze!* is Bauer's (or his narrator's) judgment of his characters. For, even and perhaps especially in the case of Baron Arthur, it is never morally simplistic or driven by obvious political motives. Indeed, despite its often-biting satire, and its vicious critique of nineteenth-century German society, *Es leben feste Grundsätze!* ultimately entails an expansive affirmation of everything human, and a desire to liberate the full range of human experiences and capacities. And, beyond its intellectual historical importance, or its contribution to the way we understand Young Hegelianism and the nineteenth century more generally, that is undoubtedly the most appropriate and lasting legacy of the work.

Translator's Note

The translation that follows seeks to be as unembellished as possible. I have occasionally added one or two words to direct the reader or keep them on track with what I take to be Bauer's intention. And there are a few bits of idiomatic and figurative language that require some elaboration beyond the strict letter of the original. But in general, Bauer's prose is mercifully uncomplicated, and I am including only a handful of footnotes, largely to explain historical-contextual details. I have retained a couple of German words or terms, partly because there is no real English equivalent, and partly to remind the reader on occasion of the novella's foreign setting. Thus, and for instance, I refer to Karl's father as "Herr Geheim-Secretair" because in English the phrase "Secret Secretary" does not really connote a governmental or bureaucratic position. Privy councillor, on the other hand, does. So, in that case I have opted to use the translation. I have very rarely included the German original in square brackets, when it seems like something crucial would be lost without doing so. For instance, I translate *Unterthan* as "subject." But in English "subject" can suggest a certain amount of autonomy or even the arbitrariness of an individual's perspective. When the narrator describes the Herr Geheim-Secretair as an *Unterthan*, however, he means the opposite — an underling or someone who gladly accepts their subjection.

There are a handful of typographical idiosyncrasies in the original that I have taken the liberty of smoothing out. For example, Bauer presents the dialogue between Karl and Arthur in the second chapter in a single block paragraph. Here, and as is conventional, I have separated each part of the exchange into a distinct paragraph. In terms of the materiality of the text, probably the most invasive thing I am doing here is publishing Bauer's contribution to the *Berliner Novellen* without Weill's. I do not have the space to comment on the implications of this omission, other than to say that they cannot be insignificant.

A Life of Solid Principles!

Part One

My dear friend,

You demand of me, almost mockingly, a Berlin novella. Perhaps you don't believe in a Berlin romance? Do you doubt whether the shallow Spree can do anything other than supply water for tea and comfort feeble souls with shallow thoughts?[1] Do you doubt whether it is capable of inviting the beautifully flagged ship of Romanticism into the exquisite realm of fantasy?

These broad straight streets, with their prosaic houses and even more prosaic faces, can they inspire any thoughts more profound than the wisdom of the city fathers, who invented the dog tax so that we might have nice smooth sidewalks?[2]

These magnificent carriages, before which we humbly remove our hats, do they contain hearts that know how to feel humanely with people? Or just fine, glittering moneybags that smile pitifully down on the empty pockets of the sweet rabble?

These bare houses, standing there like a regiment of soldiers, do they shelter spirits that burn with noble thoughts, who know how to suffer and understand a great fate, or are they inhabited only by landlords who count their money, and tenants who work to pay the rent?

Do these sandy fields bear only potatoes? Or the swaying palm of poetry as well?

This society, in which one is cold to the other, which is not permeated by any universal breath of life, can it provide us worthy material for the description of human destinies?

This city, which does not know whether it is home to a true people, or only castes, estates, and guilds, this middle ground between the property of a nation and a petit-bourgeois province, can it be the soil on which the seeds of romance prosper?

So, you ask, indeed you doubt whether we know of any interests other than those of capital, and it's bad enough that you have a right to such questions, to such doubts.

But listen, you don't need to run around with the lantern of Diogenes searching for honest people.[3] The spirit finds the spirit everywhere. Were we Berliners nothing but slaves here and there, slaves everywhere, slaves to our own prejudices, slaves to money, slaves to circumstances, slaves to the police — then indeed we should be neither worthy nor fit to be the subject of a novella, just as little as you could transfer the plot of a novella to the *Botokuden*.[4] But do not think that our spirit is nothing but a death pit, into which we throw the agony of obedience and a deadening consciousness of our constraints, and which we then fill up with a heap of vulgarity, so that arrogant tyrants can trot about on it in undisturbed pleasure, thinking that it must be so.

Everywhere you will find spirits who strive for freedom beyond restrictive chains and unreasonable circumstances, everywhere hearts that beat uninhibited, that want to sacrifice themselves in the holy fire of human love. We, too, have a society that must cultivate its characters. And where there is a society, there are victims of society, where there is a civilization there are also victims of it who are destined to bear all its disadvantages without feeling anything of its advantages. Just look at these poor cart horses of human society, who yearn to live humanely with other human beings — but the proud, aristocratic culture repels them, and the selfishness of an exclusive civilization has nothing left for them but smiling indifference or even scornful contempt. Pure romance!

So, I could tell you of many great things. The Spree always has enough water for a desperate soul to drown itself, and yet it hasn't enough to extinguish all the embers of pain, all the fires of struggle, that it indifferently flows past. Look there! What romance!

Our Kreuzberg may not be wild enough to make it the scene of a duel or even a robbery.[5] But I could tell you of duels between the rich and the poor, and of the robbery that the noble commits against the commoner. Our streets may not be dark and winding enough to make them the stage for sensational crimes. But I could initiate you into the nooks and crannies of the human heart. Romance! Pure romance!

But why should I bring the heavy artillery of a dissatisfied malcontent into the field? While I do not mind being looked at sideways [*von der Seite angesehen*] (and this fate befalls anyone who objects these days to our glorious and exceedingly splendid conditions), I will not try to stun you with too much thunder and lightning. Nor do I have the taste of the passion painters, who love to paint black on black and red on red.[6]

We hardly need to see such terrible forces in motion. We can still have enough fun together and remain good friends if we restrict ourselves to smaller terrain. Without shattering all our nerves, we can comfortably watch the stupid tricks that the heart plays on people. And you should still receive everything you wanted — a Berlin novella. And you don't have to fear that I will completely abandon our social life. On the contrary! We will only form the best judgments about it when we allow our people to talk and act undisturbed.

Remember, dear friend, we have often walked arm in arm through this city; and then you frequently said to me: "If I hadn't found you, I would have left long ago." But wait! The time has now come when I can perhaps punish you for this flattery. It is possible that I will seem as boring to you now as Berlin did to you then, and that on its own is a punishment. But then I mostly want to prove to you that Berlin is not as uninteresting as you might think. The peculiar thing about our circumstances — which are, on the one hand, almost completely rigid and lifeless, but on the other, constantly besieged by a more fleeting and livelier element — is that they are given to a certain degree of fluctuation. It may be boring if you have to live amid them; but perhaps not so much when you make them the basis of a story.

1. A Father's Curse

The old Herr Geheim-Secretair died of the times, a type of death that may one day become rampant. When you saw the old gentleman — with a face that was as humorless as a report, with a nose that had become as crooked as a signature on a petition, with a forehead that almost perfectly resembled a flat writing desk — it was hard to believe that the old man had ever been a young one. It seemed more likely that he had emerged as a file clerk from some writing-machine factory. But no, the old gentleman had once been young. But even the silly pranks of his youth predicted his future destiny. For nothing had given him greater pleasure than scribbling the words to popular songs on any flat surface he could find. His political thinking began with the Battle of Jena and was limited to mighty tirades against the French. He participated in the Wars of Liberation.[7] And upon his return, he quickly took up an office job and, knowing of nothing better to do, got married.

After giving birth to a son and a daughter, his wife died. Either the Herr Geheim-Secretair had loved her too much, or, more likely, he had been a little repulsed by marriage. For he was never married again, but from that time forward spent his life completing official documents and raising his children according to his ideals.

And yes, the Herr Geheim-Secretair did have ideals; though they were not brought down from heaven, they did not exist in the Kingdom of Nowhere, but had quite practical grounds. For he was the kind of subject [*Unterthan*] that could only be wished for. His political horizon did not extend beyond his office. He was convinced that the spirit and the destiny of a state lay in the hands of its bureaucrats. He did what he was told, never asked why, and overflowed with love and reverence for his heroic king, who had led him against the hereditary enemy and "given liberty" to the fatherland. He knew nothing of later political events or worldviews; for in the daily grind of office life there had never been a revolution.

The Herr Geheim-Secretair therefore raved about the prospect of seeing his son Karl employed as a good subject and married to the demure daughter of a coworker. How he longed to work alongside his diligent son, how he longed to talk to him in the evenings in the company of his family about the best way to assemble documents. Indeed, he was convinced that he would neglect his son utterly if he failed to prepare him for a bureaucratic career.

He had even higher ideals in mind for his daughter. He already saw her as the wife of a privy councillor, for apart from the beloved king there was nothing more venerable to him than a privy councillor. It is true that he was not so presumptuous as to assume that such a man would marry his daughter immediately. But here too he had calculated the correct course of action. A romantic office intern would surely fall in love with his daughter, who would of course be very beautiful. He would marry her as an assessor, and then, by the age of fifty, have gradually advanced to the position of privy councillor.

In these sweet fantasies the Herr Geheim-Secretair lived for a long time, and it was only after 1830 that the good man began to experience grief. He heard the terrible news that a revolution had taken place in France and that a king had been deposed.[8] Yes, yes, he said at the time, if only more documents had been written in France, they would not have behaved that way. Then he heard in his office that even in Germany people harbored a criminal desire for freedom of the press and other such nonsense, and even dared to express it publicly.

But when he heard in 1840 that in Prussia, in old, obedient Prussia, the desire for a constitution was growing, that "young screaming-souls [*junge Schreierseelen*]" were mounting an attack on the "old scribing-souls [*alten Schreiberseelen*]," he was almost struck with shock.[9] At least, he was sick from that time forward. The old wounds — the only thing he had brought back with him from France — began to torment him again, and he could no longer go to his office as regularly as he once did. Was it any wonder, then, that he gradually wasted away, and that he hated the zeitgeist that had made him ill? But how can the zeitgeist, that fabulous thing that neither employs us nor gives us food, be so impudent as to penetrate the office of an old subject and disturb him from his comfortable and submissive rest?

Oh! If only he had known that his own Karl, the Geheim-Secretair-to-be, had also been seized by the whirlwind of the times — but he would soon find out!

On that day, the old Herr Geheim-Secretair received what seemed like the best medicine imaginable for his aching legs. He had been informed that there was a secretary position open for his son. With a triumphant shout, he called out to him.

"Karl, Karl, you are safe forever! The privy councillor has assured you of his gracious protection. You must go to him straightaway and make the most obedient visit. Karl, you have a job. You can start immediately, and if you behave yourself, you will have a career. Even if things are difficult at first, I will show you the tricks of the trade. Oh, oh! It makes me young again to think of you standing behind a desk. Karl, now you can also marry soon."

But the Herr Geheim-Secretair was about to discover the monstrous fact that Karl was not at all pleased about the happy prospects being presented to him, and that he was not full of delight when he read the letter that had brought the good news.

"My God, little Clare, just look at this newly minted secretary standing before us," the Herr Geheim-Secretair declared. "My word, isn't he happy!"

"To be honest, dear father," Karl replied, "I don't really care about the news you are telling me. I simply feel no great desire within me to have a job or get married."

If the Grand Duke of Saxe-Altenberg had suddenly granted complete freedom of the press, if the King of Bavaria had abdicated in favor of a republic, if Charlottenburg had suddenly declared itself a free imperial city, the Herr Geheim-Secretair could not have been as astonished as he was by the fact that a young man could refuse an appointment.[10] Already he felt a slight trembling in his limbs, already the gout pains were returning.

"Karl, you're making me sick! Or maybe I should check to see that you yourself are healthy and in your right mind. Man, what do you plan to live on? Should the good Lord send you manna and quail out of the sky? Or will your lazy dreams give you bread? Get a hold of yourself! A good subject takes a job and writes what the authorities dictate to him. Is there anything better in life than being able to say to yourself every morning when you wake up: Today I have this and that to do, and so and so many pages to write, everything is going according to plan. You are in the office at nine o'clock sharp. You are the first to prepare your quill. And how satisfied does one feel in the evening when one counts the pages one has written, with the blissful knowledge of having faithfully served one's king. Truly! Tell me little Clare, could you imagine a nicer life?"

"I don't know, father," answered little Clare. "But I am surprised to hear Karl say that he doesn't want to get married. For I know that he only visits the privy councillor to see his daughter Marie."

"What is this I hear? You Karl, the son of a simple Secret Secretary, dare to pursue the daughter of an actual privy councillor? Well, who knows, you could distinguish yourself. You could advance up the ranks, and in ten years, perhaps you could confidently face the privy councillor and ask for his daughter's hand."

"Do not annoy me, father. Am I to honor the privy councillor just because he has a job that earns him ten times more than yours does? I know nothing of this distinction of estates that you hold to be sacred. What is a privy councillor, if he is not inwardly well-advised? And by the way, can I not happily associate with a lady without the selfish intention of possessing her?"

Up to now the old gentleman had paid little attention to his son's studies and opinions, since he would not have understood much about them in any case. He was certain that sooner or later Karl would get a job. He had no other aim at all for his son, no other plans or purposes. So what Karl was saying was completely new to him, and it frightened him.

"My son, my son, what nonsense are you talking? When I was in France, I probably heard here and there such mad talk against the sanctity of the estates and against all morality. But you must not contaminate my house with the immoral principles of the thoughtless French people. A real Prussian hates the French and knows that only wicked things come from them."

"And I, father, honor these people. You may have seen nothing in the French but a haughty, humiliated people when you entered Paris as a triumphant Prussian. You may not have noticed the pain of an oppressed nation that, despite defeats, is still striving toward the victory of freedom. But I respect this nation that in thirty years had fought more, and worked more, than the whole of Europe has in a century."

"Foolish son, you dare defy your father's reputation, you dare oppose your childish dreams and bottomless fantasies to my tried and tested experience of many years? Oh, I have wasted my life — you will accept this job."

"No father, if you want to know everything, I don't want the job. I love my freedom too much to let myself be forced into a situation for tiresome money, which everywhere can make Philistines, but nowhere a free man. I want to be human and not a beast of burden. Only the subject is paid, you think; only he receives his daily bread for services rendered. But let's see if the free man does not have within himself enough resources to get by in the world. I don't want to be turned into a machine that can be switched on and off at will, that can be left to work in the dark and that can never expect to receive the only reward that's worth the effort — the thanks of the people."

"Child, I don't understand what you are saying. I know superiors, but no people. If they are happy with me, fine, then I can be happy with myself as well. I must do what they command. And I am content when I do it properly. What more do you want? I don't understand you."

"Father, I don't think you know the new thoughts that move me. But because I think freely, I struggle, and because I am not content with this state of affairs, in which only privilege and tyrannical tutelage reign, I cannot be employed in it."

"But I want to see whether consideration for a father and respect of God's sacred rules can do nothing about your blindness. I command you, as a father, to abandon these insane views and, as befits a citizen and a subject, to accept the orderly life of an employed man. If not . . . "

"Do not threaten me father, for your threats would have as little power over me as your orders. What? Do I not also have the right to cherish my convictions? And don't I have a greater duty to myself to stick to what I know to be right than to obey an order that condemns before it even knows what it condemns? Command me to do what is right according to my beliefs and I will gladly obey you. Then though your command would be superfluous. But it would certainly not be fatherly to want to rob me of my thinking by means of a decree."

"My God! Must I put up with this? Sinner, remember God's commandments and honor your father."

"I love you, but you must also respect my views. Do not bring God's commandments to condemn me. For I cannot believe that even your God would command what cannot hold before my understanding."

That was too much for the old gentleman. Opinions that he had hardly suspected before now rushed over him one after the other. And this son, with whom he meant so well, whom he had thought destined for the highest thing he knew, a position in the bureaucracy, in whom he saw himself reflected and rejuvenated, this son dared to strike a wicked blow against everything he had venerated as sacred for his entire life. Yes, he dared to refuse the job, and knock down the tower of his hopes with a word. Shouldn't he be angry? Didn't he have to cast away the vessel that was no longer able to contain his hopes?

"If you are wicked enough not to recognize either human or divine authority, I wash my hands of you. I no longer know you. Go with your father's curse."

A few days after this pleasant conversation, the old Herr Geheim Secretair died. He died from the only strong wind that the zeitgeist ever blew his way. He died a glorious death, in defense of what had been ingrained in him as a sacred conviction. Indeed, his death was probably the most interesting and energetic thing that had ever happened to him. For he died struggling with ideas. So let us not pity him. His death was beautiful; the only event in his life that we could speak about here.

But Karl, poor Karl. His father had not even allowed him to be present at his deathbed. Only little Clare was permitted to look after the old gentleman, and he said to her shortly before his death, "You are good, my daughter, you will be fine, I bless you, and a father's blessing will have strength enough to bring God's grace down upon you."

And this Karl. He doesn't seem touched by the curse he has inflicted on himself; he does not seem to fear that the storms of heaven will shatter him; he does not walk bent over with the consciousness of being godforsaken. He consoles himself with his strength and he is proud of his arrogance!

Pious soul, fear for him! And are you not also afraid for the girl? The poor orphan. She stands alone, and her brother is her only support. But you know, pious soul, how effective a father's blessing can be. Honor your father and mother, so that your life on this earth may be long and successful!

2. At the Front Door

Is it so wrong to pursue a girl on the street? Does one have to assume that one will encounter a model of modesty who, at best, has learned a little history and French at school, and a great deal about God from the pastor, but precious little about people? — who has been made to believe that man is a ravenous beast and the cause of all sin, and that one must under no circumstances look upon him freely? As I say, one rarely has the misfortune of coming across girls who have so little natural sense that they have not risen above the limitations of their upbringing. And if one does . . . well, isn't it interesting to teach the inexperienced, and to surprise them with the realization that the male sex includes many gentle creatures who would like to melt with the tenderest affection for women.

Such were the morning reflections of young Herr Arthur, whom tailors and others in the know called Herr Baron. Heaven knows, the barons in Berlin are nearly as numerous as roof tiles; but Herr Arthur was a real, true, and genuine baron. And although his pedigree stretched back to almost antediluvian times, Arthur was either too sensible to be proud of his nobility or too clever to let his pride be seen. It is true that he had the noble passion for conquering women, but he saw very well that he could not satisfy it like his ancestors, who set out on the highway and conquered the lady of their heart with a sword or a spear. Though his old crude ancestors might have been embarrassed by him, Arthur knew very well how to assimilate modern ideas, and the modern arts of love found in him a willing pupil.

He entered the morning toilet to start his daily work — a work that consisted of doing nothing.

Incidentally, his thoughts continued, whoever the girl may be, all we really care about is entertaining ourselves, listening to ourselves, how we formulate words so beautifully, and without the least effort, utter the most excellent phrases. The girl wouldn't be stupid enough to believe them in any case. And if she were that silly — well, one only learns by making mistakes. Oh God! We have so little to do! We have enough money to live without worries, and the eternal monotony of a government job would bore us so. Why write documents? Why trudge step-by-step up a snail's path when we already occupy a comfortable position in society? Should we be thinking of science? That's nothing but rude, boisterous bickering about things that, in the end, everyone understands equally well. Or read newspapers? Ugh! We shudder to think about the long leading articles on grain reserves, or Afghanistan, or the French Chamber of Deputies. We would rather die than read a statistical treatise in the *Staatszeitung* on the population of the province of Brandenburg.[11] In the end, this kind of politics probably only exists to spoil our taste for all things political. Well, that medicine is not necessary in my case. I know from the outset that I would only be wasting my time in such fruitless pursuits. Or should we concern ourselves with poetry? We'd rather create a drama for ourselves, play the hero of our own novel.

But let's put on our yellow silk gloves and see what is happening in the street. Of course, we don't care about the faces of these men going about their daily business or these poor beggars who ask us for a penny. But there are enough girls who will or will not listen to us — and both are equally interesting.

I suspect that, like me, you will not be especially perturbed by this philosophy of Herr Arthur's. Where there is no public life, there will always be many who take life and its powers lightly. Where humanity is not respected and recognized as such, enough characters will develop who make it the object of their frivolous jokes. And poor Arthur, with all his money. From his childhood years a proud and thoughtless mother swore to him that he was an important and significant being simply by virtue of his birth. Can he then still feel called upon to make something of himself or to exercise his powers in a life that presents him with no difficulties?

That girl there, he says as he begins his day's work, that girl may be simply dressed, but her walk is too delicate, her foot is too pretty, her hand is too small to be a cook. I sense an idyll.

First, Baron Arthur imagined, there must be an old father, who has served faithfully all his life and now lives on his meager pension. And then there is his daughter, who takes pleasure in caring for him in his old age, cooking his bouillon and vegetables with her own hands, and having a modest meal with him at midday on a cleanly laid table. She also embroiders or sews something to get clothes for herself and a treat for her father on Sundays. Let's take a closer look at the matter.

It is true that she is a bourgeois girl, and Count St. Sonderling[12] would laugh and scold me for my offense against all noble beings if he saw me with her. But our society is so boring. And I really would like to see what it is like to live in this bourgeois family. We would be getting into a new situation. We could play the modest man, introduce ourselves most politely to the old man, who would be delighted to have a gentleman by his side. We would speak of the happiness of simple limitations but teach the little daughter a taste for jewelry and adornment. Repeat that pattern once or twice and — well, the rest will take care of itself.

Oh, and how pretty she is from the front. This cloth draped chastely around the neck — but wait, I am just noticing that she wears it in mourning. She is an orphan, then, whom one must support in any case and whose completely unfashionable grief must be driven away by a new feeling. And a red mouth that appears never to have been kissed! I must move closer.

"Why do you carry this basket, fair child, with these arms that are made for the weight of golden bracelets at most? How unjust that lazy men burden your tender sex with such tasks."

The one whom the baron honored with this clever flattery was none other than little Clare.

You already know that little Clare was intended by her father to be the bride of an intern, the wife of an assessor, and the elder companion of a privy councillor. Her father had always regarded her from these three perspectives alone, and he had raised her accordingly. She knew how to play the piano very pleasantly, then sit one foot prettily in front of the other and modestly cast her eyes down in front of every strange man. And unlike Karl, she had not succeeded in freeing herself from her father's upbringing. She was, as it were, already like a housewife of eight years, always dependent, always without any awareness of belonging to a larger world, always without the slightest knowledge of society. Already lost to society in advance, cut off, never knowing anything but that one day she should be the property of another, she had no longing at all to get to know the thoughts, the joys, and the sorrows of social life. On the contrary, she believed she could only preserve her immaculate morality if she did not get involved with the world at all.

But what would you expect? In this respect little Clare was like most of our girls, who are brought up, not so that they can later be independent, but so that they can be traded as easily as possible to this or that husband, like a prepared and well-preserved commodity.

Therefore, as a modest girl, little Clare could not offer the best response to the baron's question. She should have simply passed him the vegetable basket and credited his silk gloves with the heroic task of handling it. But morality, morality! For one thing, morality demands that a respectable girl should not speak to a strange man on the street, should not say to him: Sir, you bore me with your insipid chatter. No, little Clare can only turn her head and scurry away.

But Arthur wants with all his might to continue his game, so he does not mind picking up his pace as well.

"You flee from me, but your flight is so lovely that I must follow you. Can't one person love another? May he not say: I adore you? Yes, you don't want to hear me, well, I'm leaving your side, but you won't be able to prevent me from following you so that I know where you live. I'm not making any demands. I just want to stand outside your window so I might catch a glimpse of you."

Here again little Clare could have answered: "Darling, stop raving, and don't bother following me home, we live on a farm." Most of the time, however, a girl only uses her mouth to keep silent, at least on all matters worth talking about, and saves it for her stern husband's kiss. Whole houses would collapse in horror if a decent girl said something rude to an unknown gentleman in the streets.

Thus, Arthur followed her to her front door, where he tried to speak to her once again.

"Pretty child, will you leave me without any hope? Won't you tell me if I can see you again?"

By coincidence, little Clare's brother Karl was leaving the house at that exact moment.

"Dear brother," little Clare said as she hastened past, "please reject this pushy man."

A brother, Arthur thinks, this could get serious. I'll approach him brazenly.

"Good sir, your sister is very beautiful."

"And you are very pushy."

"For the sake of your beautiful sister, I will forgive your rudeness."

"What a noble soul! What generosity to chase after a girl and then forgive her brother when he defends her."

"Sir, I am a baron, and demand to speak further."

"I understand, you want to use your noble status to provoke me into a fight. But to be honest, I have no desire to see you again anywhere or at any time. Because you are rude, I am expected to give you a chance to shoot me with a pistol?"

"Coward!"

"Go satisfy your noble passions with your noble company. Shoot yourself and your peers, all of whom are as unnecessary and annoying to mankind as you are. I count my own blood too noble, my own life too valuable, to throw it on the rampart for the amusement of an idler."

"Whoa! I know the principles of a radical when I hear them. Sir, you sound like an employee of the *Rheinische Zeitung*, which I encountered the other day when my pastry chef sent me a cake wrapped in it.[13] You offend me. But please continue."

"Go dump your insipid sayings on the noble ladies, who have nothing to do all day but be bored. You may amuse them for an hour with your nauseating and thoughtless phrases. But you'll never turn the heads of our simple bourgeois girls."

"Hey, hey! It is only about seeing whether we can make these girls more receptive to the subtleties of civilization. But in any case, I thank you for your kind lesson and bid you farewell."

And with that the Herr Baron went on his way, overjoyed at all the good fortune he'd had so far that day. For one thing, he'd now sufficiently exercised his body and his mind, and breakfast would taste excellent. But he also had the whole day left to tell the beautiful story of what had happened to him. He could laugh with his friends about the character who cowardly refused to fight and awkwardly tried to lecture him on a doorstep. He could boast of his noble conduct and earn the praises of his acquaintances. And what was best, he could brag that he was about to make a new and fine conquest, capable of keeping him occupied for at least a fortnight. In short, he had a whole day's worth of chatter, twelve hours without boredom, and an intrigue ahead of him in the future. Ah, what a happy life the Herr Baron leads.

And Karl? Didn't he make himself look ridiculous, like an awkward dreamer, by blurting out his views so readily? He played the reasonable man in a society where reason, that harsh admonisher, is hardly available. And when people hear that he refused to fight, they will surely belittle him!

But despite his peculiarity, I hardly think you'll ask me how Karl got his views. His past life wasn't particularly interesting. He had been sent to school, as is the fashion, and because, in the absence of a real life, school is considered the only and most excellent educational institution. But Karl had never been a so-called exemplary pupil. He had not allowed his spirit to be captured by the mechanical hustle and bustle of school. On the contrary, he had become all the more receptive to his later principles because of the revulsion he felt toward the mind-numbing and dependent conditions there.

When his father was still alive, Karl had taken up the only profession that allows one to be dissatisfied with the existing condition: he was a writer. He had chosen the only life that allowed struggle with prejudice and oppression.

It is true the writer's status is despised in those circles where one would expect to find the greatest acquaintance with the spiritual powers of society. But they probably only despise it there because they don't understand how a man can prefer independence to a solid and untroubled occupation. But that contempt proves nothing but the spiritual weakness and hollow arrogance of those who utter it. Enough, Karl was a writer. His father had never known any-thing about it, because nothing interested him that didn't relate to the Wars of

Liberation or his office, and because Karl thought it superfluous to offend him with the news without cause.

The old Herr Geheim Secretair always assumed that Karl was working toward a bureaucratic appointment. He only received the deadly and surprising insight into Karl's opinions when he attempted to force him to accept a job.

After his father's death, Karl had a sister to support. He thus redoubled his efforts. And if our story took place in 1843, you might consider the latest Censorship Instruction to be the beginning of how the father's curse was fulfilled.[14]

3. Marie

Marie, the privy councillor's daughter, was just trying on a new hat when Karl arrived. She was so eagerly occupied she did not even notice him.

"Marie, I think the only way I will get you to look at me today is if I were a mirror."

"Angry again! And you greet me by scolding me? Ah, we girls have so little joy. You men only notice us if we are well-dressed and only speak to us to admire our appearance. And yet you want to blame us if we love the very thing that gives us your validation?"

"Marie, you're not talking seriously. You know very well that I don't give a damn about your dress, and that I'm always prepared to speak to you, even if it is not to admire a bracelet or a necklace."

"You, you, and always you. Are you the only man in the world? Do you think that all men look at life with the same coldness and temperance as you? You should have been here last night, in the company that my father invited. These handsome young men struck me as traveling salesmen, displaying their wares one after another. One was delighted by my silk dress, the other claimed that he would give half his life for a smile from me, the third spoke of the ball at court and of the new dances that he could teach me. And you would have seen me before, happily accepting all these homages like a queen. Inwardly, though, I laughed at these guests of his, who thought I had no greater purpose than to listen to their trivia. These proud gentlemen, who don't want to trouble my poor girlish mind with anything difficult, do you think that, even if I were the most famous philosopher, they would have anything more to say? If they weren't so absurd themselves, they might be able to treat women more sensibly. If only they were a little wiser, they would recognize in us women the human being who wants something higher than insipidness."

"I like you that way, Marie, but don't be offended if I worry about you. The power of ordinariness is so great. You still have your original sense; you still love your freedom and laugh at these people who think themselves irresistible because of a handsome face and a few phrases. And you would consider it a disgrace if one of these men called you his forever, if one of these cowards, who do not know how to protect their own human rights, wanted to claim an unlimited right over you. And yet! And yet! Flattery may overcome you. Selfish artistry may catch you, insipidness may dull your fresh spirit, and the philosophical girl may yet become the coquette wife of some nobleman."

"Hush, Karl, hush. Now it's my turn to be angry. How little you know me. Always allow me the pleasure of fooling these gentlemen who think they enchant me. But how can you believe that any one of them will succeed in making me such a fool that I will marry him!"

"And what do you really want, Marie? Can a woman have standing on her own these days? Is she not recognized merely insofar as she has married or is capable of marriage? It is true, your natural feeling rebels against being valued only by someone else. It seems unbearable to you to be attached all your life to a person whom you might otherwise disregard, having to respect someone whom you might otherwise despise. But won't circumstances eventually win you over? The isolation from the society in which you live will become tiresome to you, the struggle against its principles will wear you down — and there we have the wife."

"Oh, I find enough of a deterrent from marriage in you, Karl. You are not my husband, and yet you claim the right to teach me lessons like a child, and torment me with the dreams of your bad temper. Get, get! You are worth no more than all the other men."

At this moment the privy councillor entered the room. He had long disliked Marie's dealings with Karl. But he was completely under his daughter's rule and bowed to her every decision. And he could only come up with so many unobjectionable reasons for keeping him away. If you were to ask me to describe the privy councillor, you would embarrass me. His character had no prominent side, either good or bad. Yes, if I called the privy councillor characterless, I would have described him too precisely. In all his life he had had so little opportunity to think or do anything important that he was the commonplace made personal. He saw no higher interest in human life, no spiritual power, and for anything he didn't understand or didn't like, the most he did was shrug his shoulders. If this will help you get a sense of the man, I can tell you that he had the Order of the Red Eagle, fourth class, and that he could not wait for the time when he would receive that of the third class, that he greatly revered the nobility, whom he officially viewed as the pillars of the throne, and that he had acquired sufficient outward piety to be quite unctuous at times.[15] Of course, it goes without saying that he knew nothing greater and more excellent than the state he served, and that he regarded all attacks on its essence as sheer madness. He was a good company man [*Geschäftsmann*] and considered himself indispensable.

Karl was always an object of irritation for him. To him he was nothing but a proletarian who trumpeted his "high theories" to the world out of envy of everyone in a superior position and an addiction to shouting. While it is true that the privy councillor was not of nobility, he was certainly worthy of it.

At least his views of modern aspirations were narrow enough. And since he did not have the capacity to comprehend them, he despised them. But once he had achieved a level of comfort around Karl, his proud contempt gave way to condescending regret. Poor young man, he thought, I tremble for him. Isn't it a pity that he squanders his beautiful powers in such useless endeavors! He will finally consume himself and come to nothing. It is such a shame. Of course, the privy councillor never considered that he might have to endure his own hollowness or trembled at his own futility.

So, the privy councillor approached them with a smiling face and a friendly greeting.

"Rejoice with me, Herr Karl, I will soon be a father-in-law."

"How, Herr Privy Councillor, do you now have two daughters?"

"You scoff as if Marie weren't quite grown up and marriageable. Yes, yes, keep laughing Marie and scoff. But your time will come, and who knows how soon. You frivolous ones may not have seen it. But I noticed the delighted looks with which Baron Arthur followed your every movement last night. Maybe God made you two for one another."

"Well," Marie answered, "the good Lord would have to ask me first whether I wanted him to do me such a favor. I must confess that I don't care much for the baron and hardly noticed him. Dear father, you will probably have to wait a while before you become a father-in-law."

"But daughter, remember — a baron. At least show me some love and don't treat him so repulsively. As I always say: God's ways are wondrous."

Karl grudgingly gathered up his hat and left. Marie, for her part, did not think it worth bothering to disturb her father in his daydreams.

4. The Wager

It's no use, said Arthur, as he woke up the morning after the privy councillor's party. It's the only way I'm going to be able to continue living in the manner to which I've become accustomed. I've lived off my fortune to this point, but if I go on like this for a few more years, I'll be poor. The privy councillor has money, lots of money. And his daughter is beautiful. So why shouldn't I marry her? He may not be of the nobility, but he will feel all the more honored if I offer to trade my nobility for his money. His money! Isn't it right and politic for the nobility to extract the cash that the bourgeoisie acquires and use it for our pleasure? Marie is the only child. If I combine my fortune with that of the privy councillor, I'll be able to live comfortably on the pensions.

But Arthur, you getting married, that's ridiculous, and I'm sure your friends will laugh at you. What? I, who am accustomed to regarding the entire female sex as mine, I who until now spread the wing of my devotion and my lust for conquest over everything that was called a woman, I shall suddenly shrink to a silly little thing, content with just one? I, who used to own the world, shall crawl into the marriage bed and squat there as its honorable citizen? Well, who is asking that of me? The priest, whom no one has respected in ages? I'm only marrying to have money, not to get a wife. Good heavens, there are women everywhere, but money! So long as Marie is sensible and forgiving, I certainly won't be an ironclad husband!

But not so fast. She doesn't strike me as the type of girl who would readily marry just to get a man. Oh well. Am I completely without talents? It's best for me to fall in love with her a little so I can better play my role. After the wedding, everything can go back to normal. I can speak sensibly to the young woman, and I suspect we'll be able to have a fairly happy marriage.

Long live the clever and the selfish!

Arthur was too pensive today to take his usual morning walk, looking for adventures. Instead, he would visit with some friends whom he often met in the philosophical pursuit of emptying a couple bottles of champagne.

"Look here, our Don Juan," they called out to him. "Now how are you doing with that pretty middle-class girl whose acquaintance you made on the street the other day?"

Only now did he remember little Clare. Wouldn't a little adventure with her be a pleasant interlude during my engagement, he thought.

"Do you mean that chaste whore with the radical brother? On my honor. You have an antediluvian memory. I forgot her long ago."

"Excuses, nothing but excuses! We know that you can't get at her, and now you say, like the fox in the fable: The grapes aren't ripe after all."

"Leave me be, I have other, more important things to do."

"Arthur, you are making a fool of yourself. You think about important things? How rude. Go. You no longer belong in our company. And you will not be recognized again until you have finished your gallant adventure or brought it to an orderly end that can be spoken about in polite society."

"Well then! Is that a bet? In a fortnight the girl will be madly in love with me. And in four weeks she will hate me like death."

"Now that's our man! Long live Arthur! I'll bet twenty bottles of champagne, and I'll happily finish them off with you."

"Twenty bottles of champagne for a girl's honor? I fear the noble gentleman has bet too high, if he thinks such a girl's honor is worth twenty bottles of champagne. Mustn't she feel honored enough to have such a gentleman baron courting her love?"

"And Arthur, you're not going to be inhuman enough to keep this girl all to yourself. I know you'll tire of her soon. Then just say the word, and she won't be short of lovers."

Poor little Clare, be careful. Do you know life well enough to keep you from the temptations that will swirl all around you? But your father's blessing, it will protect you.

You will hear declarations of love, perhaps even be promised marriage. You will not be able to see the snake in the grass. You will be delighted to find a heart that adores you, but you will not see the malice, the machinations. You will not see the selfishness that dares to play with your feelings. But God and the blessings of your father will protect you.

Poor little Clare. And if now, ignorant of the world, you give yourself over to the blissful dream that you are loved, what fate awaits you? You will only too soon see the deception, and you will despair. Then a hypocritical comforter will come, and your heart that yearns for new love will be deceived again. And you will spend your youth in pain and pleasure, society will have no sympathy for you, yes, it will despise you because you have not respected its laws. Now you wander from one arm to the other . . . and then you grow old . . . poor little Clare . . . but the angels and your father's blessing will protect you.

But what does a person's destiny matter so long as Arthur has his fun. If only he can satisfy his whims, if only he can win his bet. Why is society such that one cannot amuse oneself except by disobeying its law? Why isn't it interesting enough to keep us from the vain games of our own selfishness? And since it gives us nothing to think about and even less to do, we might as well pursue our own pleasures. Little Clare, little Clare, think of your father's blessing.

5. Karl to Marie

I could not tolerate Berlin any longer. My departure was so quick, I left without even saying goodbye to you. And if I had to tell you why I left, I couldn't think of a valid reason. I have my main connections here in Leipzig, but I was just as able to work with them from Berlin as I am here in person.[16] So, what drove me? An inexplicable feeling of uneasiness that tells us writers that we nowhere have a fatherland, nowhere a place that we can feel at home. It doesn't really matter where we are, we are everywhere outside of society. Some despise us because we do not have a steady income, others hate us because we want to be free. People understand how one can be a carpenter, a tradesman, or a school teacher; but a writer, a pure writer, they do not understand. And that is because they do not know the spirit, because they are selfishly concerned with their own existence. They have no concept of the universal life of the people and are afraid of the public.

And we, who strive to bring thoughts to people, who seek out and speak the truth without regard to our own salvation, we who want to make the people aware of the power that lives in them and the rights that they can demand, we are treated like the pariahs of society.

As if they feared that would spread the plague among the people, they quarantine us, and only let our products circulate after they have been carefully inspected and disinfected — as if everything that comes out of our hands is unholy, and a censor must first sanctify and approve it.

If people were not so shamefully indifferent to everything that is free and high in man, if they did not live in such criminal apathy, they would recoil at a state in which thought is frowned upon and viewed as something unjustified. But no! They don't even realize that the greatest injustice is happening to them, that they too are forbidden to speak. They don't realize that we writers don't speak as individuals or bring our own thought to light — because thought does not belong to any individual. Instead, we speak in the name of thinking humanity. But they have absolutely no idea what deep, yes, tremendous meaning lies in the word *humanity*, and for this reason, they have no respect for the human being. Yes, the censor must despise the human being — not only the one whose words get censored, but also the one who is presented with only censored words.

Can you understand the censorship? I must confess that it is a power, or rather an impotence, that I find incomprehensible, as it runs counter to all aspects of life. Imagine that you had given birth to a child, and someone came to you and said: You see, dear Miss Mother, your child's arm seems to want to get very strong. It could become a nuisance to people, and what's worse, it could become treasonous. So away with it! Why, he would then continue, why concern yourself with giving birth to such children? Can't you just stay at home with the embroidery hoop? You may now reply to him however you'd like. You may tell him: Dear man, can I command nature? And what right do you have to this child that is mine? He would simply answer: The child should not only belong to you; it should also belong to humanity. And I have the job of seeing that it does not become dangerous to mankind. Do you see? Here is another dangerous place. So, get rid of it. If by this time you have not noticed that this "get rid of it" is the eternal refrain of all his explanations, you would say something like this (although it would be quite superfluous): But what kind of society thinks it can be safe with only cripples and eunuchs? Why not let every power reach its fullest development? Who does not know that the best balance of forces can only come about when you let them dominate, struggle, and harmonize with one another?

Believe me, my dear, your declamations would be preached to deaf ears, just as the most reasonable arguments for freedom of the press do nothing to alter the censorship.

Like those of the Spartans, our children are also visited in advance. But they examined their newborns to see if they were strong enough to be worthy of the name Spartan.[17] And they killed the cripples. We let only the cripples live. While everything that suggests power, effectiveness, or excitement is either mutilated or not allowed to live at all. One full of worries and forebodings, one person, is supposed to decide what is right and true, what is dangerous and not dangerous, and it is a wonder that in the end all of life does not come to a standstill.

But what is the source of all this? How is it possible to assume such a violent right over spirit that one only allows that which is impotent in spirit and has lost its spiritually procreative powers to live? It is possible that most of our social relations are now crippled and mutilated. Is there anywhere that we stand on our own feet, see with our own eyes, or speak with our own mouths? Are we recognized anywhere as reasonable, free people who might decide for themselves what is good for them, and who do not require crutches? Oh no, we are like Faust, surrounded by books, chests, and instruments. Will we not finally be disgusted by the education we have achieved, by our fabricated book learning? Will we not long to be outside, to bathe in the red glow of the morning light? But I'm afraid most will stay like Familius Wagner, who, when it is storming and raging outside, wants nothing more than to crouch behind the stove wrapped in a dressing gown, and who, instead of moving forward, never tires of reflecting on his own perfection and repeating to himself how wonderfully far he has already come.[18]

Yes indeed, right up to the stars, so far into heaven that we no longer have any sense of the earth, of its sufferings and joys, it struggles, defeats, and victories. And our efforts to set people free fail because of the people's own hard-heartedness. They don't want to hear the truth, so they mustn't hear it. But if they wanted it, oh, if they wanted it! When I consider what people could achieve if only they had the will, I do not begrudge them the oppressions they have to endure, because since they do not have the will for freedom, they are not worthy of it either.

Oh dear, Marie, I return to my old themes. I regret that I must grapple with such commonplaces every day without being able to arouse the people or drive away their indifference. I don't understand the phlegmatic ones, who let the spirit and its rights be trampled underfoot with impunity for years and are even happy with it. The censorship, it is said, is but a police institution, which is not supposed to suppress the truth, but only what is indecent, unbound, immoral, and dangerous to the state. But whoever writes without thinking, he writes the truth? A censor should be the oracle who decides on what is true and false? But what is decent? What is indecent? If, oh Marie, we kissed each other without being bride and bridegroom or husband and wife, if we kissed out of pure human pleasure, that would not be indecent according to people's common understanding. But the police would have the right to forbid us from kissing. And what isn't dangerous to the state these days? All modern states are based on the Christian order of things, or a Christian view of life. Living against this order is called immoral and at the same time dangerous to the state. So, if we, you and I, had lived in the most intimate relationship and had not thought of a Christian marriage, would we not have been traitors to the welfare of the state? O you sweet, pure Marie, do you know that people would have branded our relationship immoral and unrestrained? Do you realize, you who are so pure because you're free, do you realize that you would have been dangerous to the state?

O Marie, you are the only person to whom I am allowed to write like this, and because nature has endowed you with a cheerful and free spirit, because you have retained this spirit despite the prejudices that teach us to regard women as half human, I love you. Certainly not with a love full of sentimental and romantic sorrow, full of tearful enthusiasm: If I wanted to speak to you here about a mutual merging, about exuberant urges, about the painful joy of love, if I didn't want to acknowledge that you always must protect your freedom and independence against me, you would throw my letter into the fire, laugh at me, and forget.

But I don't know, suddenly I get a certain pounding and trembling here on the left side, which is fatal to me because it makes me sentimental. And you'll laugh at me again when I confess that my heart is beating fast because I'm thinking of the gallant Baron Arthur of whom you father spoke.

I know I can count on you, and that you won't let yourself be trafficked like other girls. If his master thinks he can conclude a marriage contract as he negotiates the price of a horse, he will find himself greatly disappointed. But there are weak hours, when one lets flattery persuade one to be loved, when one takes pleasure in dominating a man's heart, when one thinks that one can live quite well and happily with a man. Beware. You stand there isolated with your views of life. Then life assails us with its ordinariness and with its prejudices. And without our knowing it, we find ourselves with everyone else in the old and trodden track — we are overcome.

I can't get rid of these fatal fantasies. And I don't want to be sensitive. What can I say from the bottom of my heart? I know. Tell me: This wonder animal, Baron Arthur, is surely the most boring person in the world. A sweet gentleman with red whiskers and crooked legs. A man to whom you are a thousand times superior, and who is ridiculous to believe that you will submit to his genial rule. Well, I don't need to be afraid of him, he can't understand you. You might fool him for a while, but then you will let him go.

No, it's laughable, isn't it? That such a person wants to marry you, perhaps merely because your money makes a good living. O holy matrimony!

Overall, I think very little of these Berlin barons. I once had an opportunity to get to know one of them up close, and since then, as I say, I don't think much of them.

Now think of your Karl and stay true to your contempt for society!

6. Little Clare

Shortly before leaving Berlin, Karl had taken his sister to stay with relatives. Here she lived as monotonously as she had with her father, waiting for an intern to fall in love with her: unknown to the world, and of the opinion that people consisted of those who wore stockings or those who don't, those who eat lentils or those who prefer peas.

Yes, little Clare, you should get to know the world better, you should discover that there are passions other than quiet attachment to your father, pains other than the death of the old Secret Secretary. For who will initiate you into the secrets of the world?

Little Clare had never gotten to know anyone other than her father, who offered her lessons, and told her about his heroic exploits during the Wars of Liberation. Her brother had always remained something of a stranger to her. Her relatives were dear, simple people, with whom she could live pleasantly, but who could not really help her think or understand humanity.

And at the end of the day, one does become curious about humanity, which one used to let pass by with equanimity. One would like to know what this whirlpool hides in its depths. When standing by the water, one often feels the urge to jump in, a certain longing for dissolution, for devotion — a desire to unite with this enigmatic watery element. Can you blame the poor girl if she also felt like throwing herself into the human deluge that she saw overflowing in front of her?

But what of woman? Are the broader circles of action open to her? No! And so, she is supposed to find compensation in love for her husband. If woman were recognized as a spiritual, thought-filled being, she would not need to humble herself to that caprice of self-sacrifice called love for a husband. As it is, the woman is to love the only bond that keeps her connected to the world. But can one bond really compensate for an entire world? She will soon discover she has been deceived and be all the more unhappy as a result.

Arthur had little trouble finding little Clare's new apartment. He, connoisseur of girls, did not anticipate any great difficulties, especially since he heard that little Clare's brother had left Berlin. Little Clare recognized him as soon as he passed her apartment for the first time, and she looked up attentively at her window.

Little Clare felt flattered at first when she saw that she was attracting the attentions of a stranger. What delusions can take hold when we believe someone cares for us. What devotion does one not read in their eyes, what goodness of heart does one not discover in their face. And little Clare became thoughtful and began to dream only of Arthur.

Rejoice, Herr Baron, that twenty bottles of champagne are already half won.

But Arthur did not diminish his efforts. He walked past little Clare's window every day, and every day little Clare sat at that window. She remembered clearly the words Arthur had said to her that morning, and those words now struck her as exceedingly witty. The relative with whom she was living was a clockmaker, so Arthur didn't have to invent any great tricks to get in touch with her. He had enough money to buy watches, and to break something on them every day. In the course of a week, he had introduced himself to the watchmaker's family — who could not help but be friendly to such a good customer — and little Clare could now speak with him without offending custom or worrying about her reputation.

And Arthur knew how to behave. He was a perfect gentleman. He was good at telling stories. He was attentive to everything little Clare said. And he found something witty in every one of her words.

Nothing like this had ever happened to little Clare. She felt herself becoming someone new. Thoughts and perceptions awoke in her that were previously unknown. She became lively, knowledgeable, and free in her speech. Shouldn't she be grateful to the one who had breathed this new warmth into her? Didn't she have to see in Arthur the ideal of what is called wisdom, worldly wisdom? Yes, Arthur, you are loved. But do not brag about this innocent girl's devotion. You are loved because you are the first to teach her an inkling of what a human being is. You are not loved for you own sake, but because you were the means for awakening in this girl a new consciousness. Anyone in your position would have achieved the same success. For, despite what she thinks, little Clare does not love you. She loves only her own love, which inspires her to thought and teaches her to love life.

Therefore, Herr Baron, make quick use of your victory. Wake the girl from her dreams and bring her back to stark reality. For our innocent little Clare, the world with its struggles is still wrapped in the rosy scent in which love has covered it. She still sees in everyone she meets only good, dear people who, for God's sake, wish no harm to anyone. And she considers all people to be good, Herr Baron, because she sees you as the model of kindness. She is still completely delusional about life and finds nothing but vain joy and comfort in everything. But, dear baron, it would only cost you a breath, and these rosy-hued clouds would be gone. The rocky and thorn-studded paths that they obscure, the chasms over which they hover, would be revealed to despairing eyes. Skim the ethereal foam from the girl's mind, so that only the stale yeast remains.

Little Clare clung to Arthur with all the power that one loves the writer who first made us think, who first taught us our own strengths and abilities. She loved him because in him she saw the whole world, to which she had previously been indifferent, and all of society, which she had never known before.

Arthur obtained permission to take her out. He brought her to the theater, and his friends, who were sitting in the box next to them, watched attentively and congratulated him on the beautiful game he had hunted. They looked at her with victorious expressions — for there is a beauty in knowing a person's fate in advance and watching calmly as they unconsciously approach their misfortune. It is so pleasant and comforting to see from a safe vantage the abyss into which the carefree wanderer will fall at any moment. But little Clare noticed none of these mocking and triumphant expressions. She only rejoiced in the wonders of the opera, in the well-dressed crowd, and in the musical tones that roared toward her. And she was all the more grateful to Arthur that he had opened these glories to her.

The fortnight was almost up. Arthur took her for a walk under the linden trees and listened with pleasure to her declarations of love, which she never tired of repeating. Everything new that she saw, or rather everything that she now saw with new eyes, reminded her of Arthur, and it did not matter what topic she discussed, Arthur was the ultimate goal at which she arrived.

"I have beautiful paintings in my apartment, the likes of which I'm sure you haven't seen before, dear Clare. Actaeon being transformed into a stag: You may not know the old fable. Pyramus and Thisbe dying for a forbidden love.[19] Come on, we have an hour before we need to be at the theater. We can observe the paintings, and I will tell you the stories they depict."

Could little Clare fear anything from Arthur, this noble, educated man? No, she wasn't thinking anything untoward as she climbed the stairs of his apartment with him. She looked forward to his stories, nothing more. Hadn't Arthur always treated her considerately? Had he ever advised her to do anything bad? No, he only wanted what was best for her.

"Yes," Arthur concluded after explaining the fate of Pyramus and Thisbe, "yes, there is something great about two hearts that cannot live without one another. Sacrificing oneself to love is the most sublime thing one can do. Being willing to die because the world seems stale and desolate after the death of the other is the noblest deed. Do you love me so, Clare, that you can offer me everything?"

"Pardon me, Herr Arthur?"

"Clare, do you love me?"

Arthur's eyes grew fiercer, and little Clare was almost frightened. But he was so good, so kind, how could she not trust the one who expressed such noble sentiments?

"Clare, I love you, and I will perish if you don't share my feelings."

It is so flattering to see a man at our feet, to be able to smash him or lift him up with a glance, to have him totally dependent on us. Little Clare still could have left. But who could be so cruel? So, Clare did not leave.

Herr Baron, you have won your twenty bottles of champagne. Drink them up happily, and triumphantly reap the praises of your friends.

And why do you cry, little Clare? You should be happy. For don't you love and aren't you loved? You have no idea that people will laugh at you tonight, that wine-intoxicated throats will sing your praises. You have no idea that while Arthur assures you of his eternal loyalty, he thinks to himself: The fool, she made my victory very easy, and she is ridiculous enough to think that a sensible man will spend his life cooing at the feet of a tedious whore. But be happy, little Clare, because there is nothing more sublime than when one heart sacrifices itself to the other. Yes, now you are happy. You hear with delight the protestations of Arthur who thinks silently to himself: If only she were gone. You will visit him every day for the next few weeks. You will indulge in all the delusions of love. And these days of joy, which seem like a moment to you now, will later seem like eternity.

So be happy.

7. Marie to Karl

I cannot, my friend, share all the views you preach to me in your letter. I used to listen to you with pleasure whenever you spoke of such principles, because at the time they suited my circumstances and my way of thinking. Without a father who could have instilled in me respect for the male sex, left entirely to myself and my own whims, bored by people I probably didn't understand, I thought I had enough opportunity and reason not to rein in the innate stubbornness and independence of my character. I felt I was better than others. But if you think that I was very happy in this self-importance, you are mistaken.

It is a sad fate to be forced constantly to look at the social conditions in which we must live with contempt or scorn. At least, I think this task is too difficult for a woman. Ah, I have seen so many happy in their illusions, and I am beginning to suspect that illusions, and a more comfortable view of the hardships of life, are necessary for man. I knew a fool who said: "If I had no more illusions, I would shoot myself dead." I don't want to be so silly as to follow this fool and willfully seek out illusions, but I'm beginning to realize that I'm going to be bored to death, unless a mighty and enduring delusion comes over me. I don't know how I suddenly came to these views. Is it because you're not here anymore? Perhaps you have done a great wrong to leave me. As I say, I don't know.

You may be surprised to hear me sanctify these feelings, and when I justify the experience of illusions to you. But you will be even more surprised to hear that I am close to falling in love.

But hear me out. My relationship with you was beautiful, but I must confess that it was not enough to fill my entire soul. When you came into my life, I was happy. But that trembling and shaking, that almost thoughtless dissolution and devotion, which hearts are supposed to feel in the vicinity of the beloved object, that painful–pleasant state in which our mind and our mood feel satisfied, I only knew from descriptions. And you did not fail to portray this state of mind as a ridiculous and undignified sentimentality.

But you know, I think now you never loved me. Our relationship was always far too easy. Away with your ideas about mutual respect, which must consist in one leaving the other free and independent. You're asking too much conscientiousness of yourself and others — an everlasting fear of going too far in devotion. I am now of the opinion that in love one can never push devotion too far, and that respect has nothing at all to do with love.

Two friends may respect each other, they may weigh each other's good qualities, they may always be careful that one gives equal value to the other. But love neither counts nor weighs. She asks only that one give oneself completely and accept a whole in return. She does not ask whether her object should be respected. In fact, she will be all the stronger and more stubborn the less this object is worthy of respect. I can well imagine loving a beggar, a criminal, a weakling, and sacrificing everything to him with all the fire of my soul.

Heaven knows how it will arrive, but I would like to feel this for once. Your freedom, your knowledge of one for the other, seems cold and lifelessly boring to me. I long for excitement, I long for the little caprices of feeling, I long for a state in which I lose myself and find my happiness by being dependent on another from the bottom of my heart. And I am getting close to that state.

I am falling for Arthur. Your description of my would-be lover certainly doesn't fit him. He doesn't have a red beard, he's not ugly, but has a moving beauty that I (as I'm now noticing) always missed in you. He's not cold, strict, and measured like you. He knows how to cater to my petty whims and find them endearing. He is not, as you imagine, the man who approaches marriage as if it were a contract of sale. No, he seems to love me sincerely and hardly ever mentions marriage. Everything about him is charming. He doesn't exhaust himself in the usual phrases with which one can capture a weak girl's heart, no, he behaves as if women's affection for him was a matter of course. And I have a secret to confess. When Arthur began to pique my interest, I had the useless thought of wanting to investigate his character. I heard that he was often seen going out with a beautiful young girl quite uninhibitedly, which annoyed me. I got a little colder toward him, and he might have noticed something. But when, by chance, I brought up the subject of him and his close associates in conversation with one of his friends, he could not do enough to describe Arthur's kindness. For example, he supports with money and gifts a young woman, an orphan with no elders, in whom he has no romantic interest. And the girl adores him like a father precisely because he is completely disinterested. So, my suspicion was unfounded, Arthur shows himself to be a noble and excellent person here, too, and I have an injustice against him to correct. But that only excites me more — and I confess, I am trying to please him.

Enough, you may call it weakness, you may call it feminine capriciousness, you may even call it nonsense, but I only want love.

And what if I should marry now? I can hardly understand what you have against marriage, nor can I understand why I ever laughed at it. You will respond: Marriage is not a free relationship because it is based on belief in the sanctity of its arrangement and not on mutual trust. But in this manner, you could dissolve all human relationships with the acidity of your doubt and the fanaticism of your freedom. And if you wanted to be consistent, you would ultimately have to retire to a desert island, just so as not to have to enter into any human relationships.

Why shouldn't feeling, why shouldn't sensation also have their rights? Feelings and sensations are the only bonds that can hold two people together. How could two people merge together if they faced one another with pride and freedom, each only ever wanting to be self-sufficient? And marriage is a union accomplished more through obscure feelings than cold calculation and mutual consideration of characters.

I may be wrong, I may be raving, I may no longer be able to consider the circumstances and — to use your favorite expression — to criticize. But leave me my delusions in which I feel happy, don't wake me from my enthusiasm, which warms me. Leave me with the belief, which I have come to accept, that people are there to be guided and determined by circumstances, rather than constantly criticizing and thinking, and never finding peace of mind.

And I want to rest. For once, I feel quite inclined to trust. I don't know what has come over me, but I'd really like to play the tyrant over this Arthur, and to make him realize that he's not allowed to love anyone but myself.

And then, tell me, can we poor women ever count for anything in society other than through men? Yes, we are only allowed into the world as fully realized and independent if a man puts his weight behind us, to whom we then of course must relinquish our independence. I don't know if we require this support by nature, but under the current social circumstances, that is the way it is, and I am in the process of making peace with it.

Of course, this line of thought alone would not be enough to make marriage acceptable to me. On the contrary, I consider it not only pleasant but beautiful to endure life and its dangers in the company of a man. Here I believe I have found the relationship in which the sanctity of my feeling is also respected, because it is secured by a firm commitment that it will not be deceived, desecrated, and trampled on. Here I have the union of two souls who promise to endure one another's whims and make space for one another's feelings.

Please do not come at me with your criticism. Criticize books as much as you like, but the kingdom of your goddess must not expand further.

I may, in your opinion, have become the victim of ordinariness. I may be deceived and mastered by circumstances, I may let the tyrannical demands of feeling mar the calm of my mind, I may be wrong in trusting too much, but I am comfortable in my sentimentality, and you cannot tear me away from it.

Farewell! I can only hope that you will soon console yourself by falling in love out of revenge.

8. The Suitor

Arthur isn't really that bad. We would be mistaken to call him an evil man, and you would not be so weakhearted as to find him repugnant. Be honest, you also don't think much of those wondrous beasts of wickedness that you can travel to the Leipzig Fair and see for a couple of pennies.[20] Arthur doesn't have a malicious heart. But he must have fun, he must give his life, which is otherwise so comfortable, some variety. And can you blame him for being selfish? Perhaps he was once a person with many talents. Perhaps in his youth he raved about Schiller's *Robbers*.[21] Under different circumstances, he would have become a good and pleasant citizen of the state. But can he be condemned if no opportunity to act valiantly and selflessly presented itself? Believe me, people are never bad by nature. They only become so when circumstances fail to deprive them of their selfishness and inspire them toward a universal purpose.

Arthur is quite agreeable and amiable in company. His friends — and he has real friends — love him because he knows how to live and is never boring. They would laugh at me if I said: Beware of him, he is a bad character. They would respond: We wish we could all live as carefree as him, and basically have one and the same principles.

Arthur doesn't have a great deal of in-depth knowledge, but he has a talent that makes up for it. He knows how to read people and approach them from the right direction.

He can converse very pleasantly on all sorts of topics, and if you are eloquent and penetrating, you can interest and inspire him for many things. He doesn't want stiff dignity. Serious moderation is ridiculous to him, and he is convinced that life is not worth making a fuss over.

Mind you, he did seduce poor little Clare and who knows how many other girls! But good heavens, does that set him apart from the rest of the world? He toys with women's honor and with their peace of mind. If only society would make the physical innocence of women the object of its frivolous contempt. But no, the same society that is so strict and hypocritical about outward honor feels no shame trammeling underfoot the honor of our reason and the freedom of our spirit. And it is bad enough that a girl's honor, the purity of her soul, is sought merely in her virginity.

Yes, Arthur is not faithful, and what is worse, he knows beforehand that he will not be. Well, all the better, he will be able to be colder and more independent in all circumstances. And fidelity, fidelity! What a sentimental word! What if it was the girl who was not faithful, but he clung to her enthusiastically? Isn't it better for him to be inaccessible to any deception from the beginning? He, by the way, will know what fidelity in love is all about — that it is nothing but a torment that one afflicts on one's own heart and on the heart of others, a torment that tries to capture the first moment of loving excitement and extend it to eternity, a torment that wants to make all decisions, all actions of our entire future, dependent on that one moment in which we surrendered ourselves to the deception of love.

Then you might come with the flat reproach that he wants to marry for the money. But surely that's the general fashion now, and Arthur doesn't claim to be any better than the time in which he lives. If he pretends to be in love with a girl while courting her money, that is only proof of the goodness of his heart. He respects Marie by not presenting his soul to her in its nakedness, and it certainly makes her feel flattered and happy if he can persuade her that he loves her for her own sake.

So, you won't be angry with my Arthur, you won't envy him when you hear that he's been very lucky with Marie.

And he is lucky. Little Clare let him bewitch her because she didn't know the world. Marie loves him because she thinks she knows the world too well. And yes, Arthur is even luckier than you might think. For he has the great advantage of having actually fallen a little in love with Marie.

Arthur noticed at once that he would have to treat Marie differently than the women he was used to dealing with. He saw that she was making an effort to adopt a steadfast and masculine philosophy, and he reflected that in his operations. He knew what a great potential for coquetting women had. It was only a matter of bringing out this disposition in Marie and making her receptive to the trifles of sociability. How interesting it was to surprise this girl with the discovery of the weaknesses that lay dormant in her character, to make these weaknesses dear to her feelings, to put the spirit, which is tired of thinking and judging, to sleep, and to sit in its place the pleasant rocking motions of sensitivity, the feverish excitement of the heart. Arthur fell in love with this task of his, he fell in love with Marie because she gave him cause to be active and to exercise the cunning of his mind.

Marie had raved about society with Karl in metaphysical reflections. She had believed herself strong enough to avoid the temptation of being gently carried along by the stream of ordinariness. So, she could scarcely notice it at first when she got ready to swim in that stream as well.

Arthur wasn't pushy. True, he knew how to arrange it so that he came to the house of the privy councillor almost every day. But he did not immediately stand before Marie with the demand: Do you love me? At first, he kept his distance from her. For he knew that her attention would be drawn to the one who was original enough not to place himself among the other worshippers.

"I know of nothing more ridiculous," he once said, "than a lady who despises ornaments; but just as ridiculous is to live for the sake of them. Is the beauty that nature has given us such a small commodity? And is it not an ingratitude to nature to disregard her gift, if we do not embellish and cherish it as much as we can? No matter how strong my spirit may be, I cry out to those around me: Delight in my real attributes, not in my tinseled state. But it is also good if I give the beautiful content a beautiful form. Participating in cheerful sociability demands that I also take the eyes of others into consideration."

Marie could not disagree entirely, although she quarreled with him over his claims. But it was only a small step from teasing to a more heartfelt interest. The next evening the baron remarked that Marie seemed much more adorned today than previously.

This first success made him bolder. He drew ever closer to Marie, and while he initially appealed to her way of thinking, showering her with commonplace sayings that resembled noble thoughts, he soon found this proud manner of conversation tiresome to her. He then went on to more tender speeches. But how can one describe the course that so-called love takes in a heart? Is it a mere thought that can be developed? Is it based on assumptions that can be intellectually set forth? No, it is there, suddenly and without reason. It claims its right simply by existing. And it would be a bad love that wanted to justify itself through reasons alone. Love is in no way rational. It is a power that expands our mood, a power that, through the obscure excitement of feelings, captures the clarity of spirit.

In any case, Marie soon imagined that Arthur was the only man in the world with whom she could be happy. Those delusions and excitements that she longed for had finally found her.

Could she have wished for anything more?

9. Karl to Marie

Well, that was fast! Marie, I must accept that you don't love me anymore. For where would I find the right to complain? You have your free will. How can I bind it? Constancy and fidelity are nonsense. We may think it possible when, carried away by the first strength of a feeling, we forget all time, all change. We may make promises then. But such a promise cannot bind. Do the transformations that take place in our spirit lie within the sphere of our calculation? Can we determine the new views that life brings us in advance? Can we set a limit on them? And just as our spirit is constantly changing, so our feelings will also change. We will learn to look at people we used to love from different directions. In short, it is impossible to be faithful. Only the lover who turns himself into a Robinson Crusoe, who excludes himself from all society and its influences, can be faithful.

I don't want to blame you for falling in love again, and in a very special way. But that you believe in the constancy of this love! And you want to marry! This is unbearable. And it is more unbearable that I feel there is no longer any way of saving you. You won't hear me when I tell you: Marie, think about it. I can only refer you to the experience, and by then it will be too late.

Oh, if you could only hear yourself speak. You don't know how much sorrow your little letter has caused me, not because of the event it recounts — I was prepared for that sooner or later. No, because I saw from this letter how much your strong and clear mind is already affected by "accidental feelings" — as you yourself say — and how you make a vain effort to justify your current state of mind before the reason of a sensitive thinker. If you could read your letter with complete impartiality, like that of a third party, you would soon convince yourself of the baselessness of its claims.

And here I come, despite your prohibition, with my criticism. I have a duty toward you, and I must warn you again, if only to ease my conscience. You yourself admit that love does not look at the personality of the one to whom it is directed. And yet you want to say you love Arthur? You love this person, Arthur? This person, to whom you want to tie yourself by an almost inseparable bond, despite the fact that you say that he is something insignificant in your love? So again, you say you love Arthur. No, you're merely infatuated with the state of mind that's new to you and that you're coddling like a newborn child. Until now you had not known the strength of your feeling. You were surprised, perhaps delighted, when it asserted its voice. And now you imagine it is everything. Arthur becomes the ideal in your eyes, but only because you don't want to disgrace your feelings by favoring an ordinary man. You are convinced that Arthur loves you as well, of course, for how could this soul-magnetism in which you are now infatuated not be strong enough to attract and fascinate another heart, how could this soul-electricity not impart itself with all its might to Arthur's spirit? In this manner, you fool yourself, and it's still very doubtful whether Arthur really loves you. Yes, I even hope he doesn't love you. You will be angry with me, you will perhaps throw my letter away now, but please keep it and read it again in three months' time.

Yes, yes, I hope Arthur doesn't love you, so at least he'll take a colder view of your relationship, and thus be able to protect you from a melting and unnerving sentimentality. Then you will be spared a great torment. For there is nothing more terrible than two souls who, carried away by the blindness of their first feelings, finally come to rest and get to know each other, and see each other inhibited, bound, and tortured by the mutual demand for fidelity — two people who are not strong enough to bid their delusions be gone, and who think it their duty to torment each other by demanding a feeling that can neither be obtained by force nor, when gone, by force retrieved. What infinite boredom will the two see before them, in what unworthy hypocrisy will they be compelled to live out their lives, in a situation where insight always comes too late.

But if Arthur doesn't love you, if he intuits your state of mind from the outset, he may succeed in gradually calming you down. And when you finally wake up from your dreams, you will certainly be overcome with great boredom and exhaustion, like all those who have recovered from a fever. But at least this boredom will be painless and without any torment.

O Love, love! You yourself admit that it is a great illusion, and that in it the capriciousness of feeling is allowed great preponderance over the insight of the mind. Well, play with her, but don't use her as a bond for a relationship that is supposed to last until death. Is it right then that a union for life should begin with an illusion, is it right that a whole institution, such as marriage, should be founded on deceit?

And you may still claim that the human race needs deception, you may say that cold knowledge and judgments are boring. And perhaps with this you capture the majority of people, who are too lazy to think for themselves. But you don't capture the free man. Yes, it is true, most people live for the day. They are slaves to the conditions inherited from their parents, and their anxious mind sanctifies these conditions. They find their position tolerable because they cannot think of any other, or because they consider change impossible. But it wouldn't be worth living if we had to tell ourselves at the end that all life had been nothing but a comedy, that we had taken prosaic canvas for rosy clouds, that everything, both nature and spirit, was but dust and wind, and the greatest heroes were only the worst screamers and braggarts. Believe me, only he who feels himself weak seeks deception, and in order to cover up his own weakness he ascribes it to the whole human race.

Those who cannot overcome momentary upheavals often sacrifice their entire happiness in life, and you are about to do the same. You want to get married. Do you think that, out of a state of affairs such as marriage, which will soon enough prove a terrible bondage, one can make a deception that lasts forever? No, the pure poetic aroma of sensitivity, in which you now see everything, will soon dissipate. And nothing will remain but the pale, oppressive prose — a terrifically boring wasteland, the limits of which you will only have reached at the end of your life. Still, you believe that Arthur is different than he really is. You let yourself be lulled by the fantastical tricking-tones of love. But what if Arthur is not the man to savor the whimsical happiness about which you rave? When you wake up now, when your spirit calms down again, won't you curse your mood and at the same time feel disgust at the one who has caused you to deceive yourself? Won't you take him for an intruder who had the gall to sneak into your heart wearing brilliant, false garb? But you will not consider that it was you who lent him this robe.

And — oh it is unbearable — you will be chained to this man forever, yes, a certain demand of your heart, a certain consideration for the peace and comfort of your soul, a desire to keep your mind fresh and free, will force you to obey the man whom you would rather hate and whom you would like to avoid. It is possible for you to settle into the situation, it is possible for you to appease the regrets of the heart and the bitter thoughts of the mind. But that will only slow things down a little and, like so many fellow sufferers, you will persevere by pulling on the same wretched and oppressive yoke. And again, free spirit will be crushed and lost to humanity.

You still imagine that in Arthur you have a man whom you can lock up like a little bird, tease, and ask that he should not concern himself with anything but you: because your little heart and "the sanctity of your feeling" would be jealous of everything that might occupy his soul. Arthur shall serve you continually, as a hearth on which you feed the fire of illusions, as a jar from which you constantly draw new deceptions.

But you must consider that you are degrading Arthur with such a demand. A man, at least a sensible man, has more to do than keeping a lady in love. Life offers him higher interests than indulging the selfishness of another, and you must know that, in the end, even you would find an unchanging devotion, an eternal hallelujah, singing the sanctity of marriage and the bliss of fidelity, unbearable.

So, what do you actually want with your praise of a relationship in which, as you say, consideration is given, not only to simple knowledge, but also to the contingencies of feeling. Precisely because the sensation is accidental, the bond that is tied through it should also be merely accidental. Sentiment should not make us slaves of another. We should always keep open the opportunity to loosen the bond as the sensation subsides. And whence comes your sudden hatred of "cold knowledge"? Oh, if only people knew, their knowledge would certainly not be cold. It would push back the feelings that always want to become overpowering, that always want to make us dependent and unfree, into their proper limits. People would not be slaves to conditions, but conditions would be dependent on people.

And Marie, just answer me one question. You are not yet so in love that you do not want to defend your love, your feeling has not yet blinded you so much that you should not at least wish that all people would share the same blindness with you. But now tell me, with what do you want to defend yourself, with what do you want to blind me? By scorning the strict reason that sees sharply everywhere. By saying that you don't want to know anything about a cold deliberation. Marie, Marie, can a relationship be good if one must throw oneself into it without hesitation, if one can only affirm it by denying reason?

So, I've written and written, and I'm afraid I've been preaching to deaf ears. I have told you in advance all the experiences you will have. But I suspect that I have just described it to you in vain, just as it will be in vain if you realize it too late. Oh, that you, too, had to fall into the trap that society casts upon all free souls. The lessons that society teaches usually come at the wrong time. It will teach you lessons too, but you won't be able to use them. Perhaps you will be saved one day from the delusion you are in now, and that might make your mind sharper. But society will demand of you that you persevere in sacred deceit, it will forbid you — unless death intervenes — ever to fall in love again. You loved me, now you love Arthur. Maybe there will come a time when you will say you loved Arthur, and now . . .

So once more Marie, think about it.

10. Two Letters

Arthur to Karl

Good Sir,

My bride has instructed me to return the enclosed letters that you wrote to her. We have read and heartily delighted in them. Yes, we are grateful to you, because you gave us an extraordinarily enjoyable few hours. However, Marie thinks that continuing to write her long letters would cost too much of your time. She would also like you to know that she is very happy and will be marrying me in just a few weeks.

Arthur

***

Arthur to Little Clare

Dear Child,

I hope you will read the enclosed with peace of mind. Call me a scoundrel, nefarious, a perjurer, but tell me honestly: Do you really believe in loyalty, and that you would have remained faithful to me? Since it was not possible for us to love one another forever, is it not best for us to be open with one another and get through the pain of separation sooner rather than later? Imagine, then, that we were joking and forget me. I am not worth thinking of or even seeing one more time.

Arthur

***

Enclosed was nothing more than a simple card on which the happy Marie and Arthur announced their engagement.

I don't know whether little Clare fainted or wished to die. All I know is that at first, she thought it was a hoax, and that she only became convinced of the truth after she had gone to Arthur's several times and been turned away.

Don't be afraid that little Clare will throw herself into the water in despair. It would be too simple to eliminate a person and end our story in a tragic and nerve-racking way.

It's not so easy to die, by the way. And what would life be if you wanted to throw it away after every failed love affair? Little Clare was, of course, a woman who had given herself up for the first time, and a girl who adored the one to whom she had sacrificed "her everything." So, at first, she wept a lot. She also felt quite ill and found it difficult to walk or stand. But in the end, you console yourself, you look at things more resolutely, yes, the pain makes us all the stronger once it's over. And in the end, you must learn from experience.

But with little Clare, there was one particularly bad possibility. For she sensed that she was going to become a mother. And then wouldn't she have to reveal the matter to her brother? Karl had written to say that he would soon return to Berlin. And what would he say now?

11. The Wedding

"Me, mad at you little Clare? Why? You truly did not dishonor yourself when you followed the inclination of your heart. No, I respect you, because your love was whole and complete. It was not selfishness that drove you to Arthur, and you ought not mistake me for a pedant who makes silly, philistine speeches against acts of passion. No, little Clare, I am not angry with you."

"Karl, my brother, you lift me up and ease the pain that torments me. For although I have been deceived, you do not consider me impure."

"What does pure mean? What is impure? Tell me, little Clare, haven't you become more sensible, and hasn't contact with the world clarified your senses? You will therefore understand me when I say: The world never defiles us, if only we do not let it overwhelm us, if only we do not let the defeats that we suffer in it defeat the strength of our spirit. We always remain pure so long as we are not lured into foolish self-forgetfulness, be it in joy or in sorrow. You loved, little Clare, you gave yourself, and that is beautiful. I respect you more than if you tormented yourself with brittle modesty. You've been cheated, it's not your fault. You were still unable to see the contemptible hollowness of the heart, which you believed to be filled with noble and great sentiments. You've been made wise, and in the future, won't let yourself be captured so easily."

"Karl, what kindness. But I'm afraid you'll be much more upset when you consider who it was that betrayed me."

"Oh, little Clare. If this Arthur clung to you with a sensitive and passionate disposition, if he had failed just as freely as you, I could not be angry with him. His fault would also only be a fault of the heart, which the cool spirit does not have to punish. But he certainly calculated his deceptions from the outset. He wanted to spoil you with a wrinkled and sneering smile. He dared to sacrifice you to his noble pleasure, to use you as a means to bring some variety to the wasteland of his ignorance. And what he has done in cold blood will be avenged in cold blood."

"You scare me, Karl. Oh, don't be too hard on him. Remember that I loved him. And if you cannot have pity on him yourself, have pity on that which your sister appreciated in his company. Besides, if you expose him as unworthy, don't you belittle me as well, as I was so incapable of seeing through him? And aren't you also putting yourself at risk?"

"Be still, little Clare. Neither our circumstances nor my thoughts point toward bloody revenge being taken here. We can only expose the worthlessness of this fop. And we don't just owe it to ourselves. Isn't it our duty to save Marie who is still my friend despite her current lovesickness? Who knows what arts he used to cloud her clear mind and to prevent her from seeing the inner hollowness beneath the outer splendor. Is it true that you girls always choose to fall in love with such hollow subjects? But Marie is not just in love, she also wants to get married. If I were a complete stranger to her, I would still have to show her whom she wants to associate with for the rest of her life. Maybe I'll succeed in awakening the old spirit in her — to show her the hollow ground on which she is standing, and snatch at least one victory from that selfish and conceited baron."

When Karl arrived at the home of the privy councillor, he discovered a large company there. He learned that it was the day that the baron and Marie were to be married. Marie was not available, as she was busy in her toilet getting prepared. And she probably would not have felt like listening to a long sermon about Arthur in any case. Karl thus demanded to speak to Arthur himself. He was led into a room alone and, after a long wait, the baron entered with a beaming face.

"My apologies," he said, "there is much to do when preparing to enter holy matrimony."

"Do you not recognize me, Herr Baron?"

Only then did Arthur take a closer look, and it was not difficult for him to make the connection.

"Oh look, it is Herr Karl, my bride's intimate friend. Well, I am glad that you do not disdain to honor me at today's festival. But don't bother, I've had the opportunity to get to know you personally before."

"Do you really think I came to watch you sacrifice a friend's fate to your whims, maybe even your selfishness? No, I prefer to stay away from such festivals where youth, freedom, and beauty are offered up to the uncouth husband of prejudice and smothered passion. But can't you think of anything for the sake of which I should disturb your joy today?"

"What would that be?"

"Good sir, I have a sister."

"Yes, by heavens, she told you how unlucky we were in our love. But I must say, today is not the time to talk about these things. Come back later. I am prepared for any satisfaction."

"No, today is perhaps the one day when I can avenge little Clare and her mistreated heart. Wretched one, you have desecrated my sister's reputation. You used her inexperience and mockingly played with her heart, and you dare speak to me about a marriage you wish to celebrate today."

"But sir, what do you actually want? You, who think so little of marriage, cannot have come to force me to marry your sister."

"No indeed! I respect little Clare too highly to wish her a companion for life. But the insult you did to her taught me your character. And I cannot allow that you, who are so disrespectful of humanity, who think that human beings exist only to gratify your noble desires — I cannot allow that you are also deceiving Marie today, who in the blindness of her love has not yet gotten to know you, but who should know, through me, who she has in you."

"Me! Insult little Clare? I had no such intention. Little Clare loved me, she gave herself to me, and a strong spirit like yourself should not find anything unusual in this. Little Clare may have been innocent, but in your eyes, innocence is of no value compared to the hour in which we lose it. Little Clare was happy when she loved me. She was wrong about me, but my God, how much fuss can one make of that. Is it not a common fate for one person to be deceived about another? It is enough that I made little Clare happy for two weeks."

Karl had to listen to all this quietly. What should he do? Should he pounce like an enraged beast on the one who tormented him, tear out his heart in cold blood? He would not have achieved his goal, and he would have been shamefully thrown off the premises. His soul twisted and withered under the kicks of Arthur's words. But Karl could do nothing but furiously regret his own weakness.

"Little Clare," the baron continued, "may be pregnant. Fine, that is not a big deal. I'll have enough to keep her and her child from starving."

Karl had made up his mind.

"No, honorable Herr Baron, don't assume that Little Clare will have a child. I didn't come to beg you for alms. That would only insult the child that little Clare carries under her heart. If it gnawed at the crumbs that fall from your table, if it fed on the savings taken away from the children of the legal marriage bed, it would forever bear the shame of being dependent on such a father. So, calm down. You will never know anything about little Clare's children. But perhaps I can still make it possible for you never to climb into the marriage bed of which you seem so certain."

Karl stormed out to the sound of the baron's laughter.

Basically, he's a good fellow, thought Arthur, but it's his misfortune that he takes things too seriously and that he everywhere wants to act on principles. Hey, isn't all of life a game and isn't the greatest enjoyment in not calculating but waiting with laughing courage to see what the next day will bring. But with this Karl, everything must follow a formula. He conjures up a framework that he calls humanity, and then seeks to bring everything within it. And so, it cannot fail, he must lose out every time. If he did things our way, like other people, the matter would be decided instantly — we would shoot one another with pistols. But no, that too is against his principles. Well, I am curious how he plans to prevent me from marrying.

And with a happy heart he went to see whether Marie was finally finished getting prepared.

A large crowd of guests had gathered for the bridal party, and it was easy for Karl to mingle with them unnoticed. He had the pleasure of listening to their witty remarks.

"The privy councillor has incredible luck," the court councillor said. "He has advanced, and it is not even clear how he's done it. And now he has a rich baron as a son-in-law. My Rosaline is pretty enough. She plays piano like Liszt, writes verse like Goethe, and sings like Löwe, but no baron has come to her."[22]

"The privy councillor is said to have a great deal of money," the captain replied dryly.

"I see what you are saying," the court councillor answered, "these days people consist of nothing but moneybags. But shouldn't there be more soulful hearts that consider what is inside and not merely the shiny outside? I tell you, my daughter is very well educated."

"I do not doubt that for an instant, dearest court councillor. But education is so cheap these days, it will soon come rushing toward us at every turn. And my feeling is it's rather passé. Money, money, that's the only thing that maintains its value while everything else gets more expensive."

"You have no soul, no heart, Herr Captain. Our time still knows feelings. For example, devotion to our beloved monarch, obedience to our superiors, humility before God, do these things count for nothing? Oh, I do not despair for our time, there must still be loving hearts. Rosaline will have a husband."

"Well, it could be worse," the captain concluded. "At least the court councillors have not become world-weary."

"I don't understand the baron," said the cavalry captain next to the major. "His bride isn't all that beautiful, and she's said to have all sorts of whims and caprices, so why does he marry this girl who's not even a noble?"

"No now," remarked the major, "with all their money they will be able to live all the nobler."

"The baron," said the banker, "is said to have a very noble character. He always pays his debts. Miss Marie will be quite happy."

At that moment the bridal couple entered; Karl examined Marie closely. He had not changed his opinion, and he assumed there would be some trace of sadness in her face, some premonition of the misfortune that awaited her. But there was none, and her face seemed to glow with radiant delight as she stared at Arthur who stood beside her, the embodiment of love and gallantry.

The bridal couple was approaching the door when Karl jumped forward to block the bridegroom's way.

"I have come," he declared, "to object to the marriage that is about to be contracted."

Arthur smiled calmly, held his spectacles in front of his eyes, and said, "Who is this person who appears to have escaped from an asylum?"

"My God it's Karl," Marie said. "Has his inflexible hatred of marriage made him mentally unstable?"

"Outrageous," shrieked the privy councillor.

"A remarkable specimen," the court councillor chimed in.

"Perhaps he was also speculating on Marie's money," remarked the captain.

"Was I mistaken about the character of the baron?" asked the banker.

"This noble baron," Karl continued, "seduced my sister Clare and then scornfully tossed her aside like an unwanted toy. Marie, I warn you for the last time."

"Do not listen to him," Arthur told Marie. "I do not know him or any Clare and I truly don't know what could possess him to slander me so."

"You are a vile man, Herr Baron!" shrieked Karl. "You dare deny to my face what you admitted in private a half hour ago?"

"My good stranger," the baron replied, looking contemptuously at Karl, "if you've come here to upset me, you will fail. I can see that you are not sane. If you were, I should punish you for choosing such an inappropriate place and time to insult me. Go now, or I'll find some means of getting you out of the house."

"Exactly," the privy councillor happily agreed, "I will have the servants called. Who are you to enter this house uninvited and, with the most shameful slanders, disturb a celebration at which only love and unity should be present. Away with you now, or else."

"There's no need for more threats," Karl said. "I see you don't want to hear me. Yes, you have the power here, privy councillor, and I must yield to it. You are a respected man Herr Baron, and you alone must be believed. I should have left a long time ago, for I must have known that nothing can ever be done with lovers and selfish people. I take my leave, knowing that I have fulfilled my duty."

And thus, it was once again Arthur the dreamer's turn to laugh at the enthusiasm of Karl the radical.

"The carriages, the carriages, to the church," the privy councillor cried. "We won't let this nonsense disturb us, will we dear daughter."

And they got into the carriage.

"What a strange man," the court councillor said to the captain next to him. "Young people these days, what a mess they are causing. I know the source of it. It's the liberal principles that make their heads spin. They all want to be who knows what, to represent something, and then they fall for such antics. Oh, the times are bad! No one has a mind or a heart any longer. All these young people — they make me wish my Rosaline doesn't marry after all."

"But suppose that the young man had been right," the captain remarked.

"My God, Herr Captain, what are you thinking? The Herr Baron is such a noble and great character, and he was not the least disturbed by the episode. Oh, I admire the calm Herr Arthur displayed when confronted by the young man. Yes, the Herr Baron has both a mind and a heart."

"In any case," the captain concluded the conversation, "even if the odd man had been telling the truth, he said it in such a ridiculous manner. How could he think that anyone would listen to him? He seems to me to be a fanatic who knows nothing of the world and only appears in it to make a fool of himself."

"A peculiar story," the cavalry captain said to the major. "I don't think the baron is as innocent as he looks. Nevertheless, he did not betray his aristocratic nature, but behaved like a real nobleman throughout."

"I still have to laugh," replied the major, "that this man believed he could undo the marriage because the baron once had the fun of seducing a bourgeois girl. As if that doesn't happen every day. I have nine daughters, but on my honor, if they all had bridegrooms like the baron, I would have no difficulty giving them away."

***

"You are so thoughtful, Marie, my dear bride," Arthur said on the way to the church. "Is it possible that at this solemn moment any suspicion of your Arthur could stir in your pure soul?"

"Arthur, dear Arthur, I know you are innocent. But I feel sorry for Karl. His principles, his inexplicable abhorrence of marriage, and perhaps also his love for me have driven him half mad. Is it not terrible that he slandered even his own sister just to keep me from this marriage?"

"Yes, Marie, this person is criminal. To slander me in your eyes — as if, while courting you, while you alone were all I thought of, I could have occupied myself with any other girl. But he shall not escape his punishment."

"That is just what I fear, dear Arthur. But if my love has any power over your heart, if you will grant me only one request today, forgive that poor man. Do not pursue him any further, attribute what he has done to delusion and excitement, and above all remember that he was once dear to me."

"Noble soul, can I be angry with him any longer if you forgive him? Yes, let's leave him to the punishment he carries in his conscience. The disgrace he has caused himself today will be sufficient revenge. Let's not think about him anymore."

"Arthur, dear Arthur, I was not mistaken in you. Yes, you are the ideal of the noble, good man that I so often met in my dreams but always despaired of finding in reality."

Is Marie not very happy? And if our friend Arthur succeeded in keeping her in her deceptions to the death, if he was able to keep wearing the mask behind which he is now hiding after the wedding, wouldn't Marie be happy? What she hoped for has come to pass. She is nourished by an illusion.

***

Little Clare had been seized with a great unrest when Karl left her. She pictured the many dangers her brother faced. His temper will carry him away, she thought, he will make a wrong step. Oh, I would have preferred to remain completely silent.

Instead of suffering at home, she went out into the street, wanting to keep her eyes busy to calm her mind. She soon arrived at a church with a large crowd gathered in front. Oh God, she thought, it's going to be a wedding. Maybe the bride is happier than me. Maybe she's entering into the bond that she's longed for. I must go. This is no place for the brokenhearted.

She was about to turn back when a magnificent carriage full of adorned people drove right past her. In it sat Arthur and Marie. Poor little Clare. Instead of being thrown flowers by the happy bridal couple, she was showered with the dirt and mud that the carriage picked up from the road. Poor little Clare!

But an inexplicable curiosity drove little Clare to go back to the church. Did she want to compare Marie's happiness with her misfortune? Did she want to intoxicate herself with the pain that would tear her apart when she opposed the love sanctified before the altar with her scorned and mocked love? I don't know. But I know this much, little Clare did not need to feel any envy. Because what she witnessed was nothing other than the greatest desecration of love she would ever know.

Marie loves Arthur. Fine, but society doesn't allow her to make that love a reality. Every girl must be content with a half-hearted sensitivity, with no opportunity either to test herself and the lastingness of her feelings, or to get to know the person she thinks she loves. And there we have the bride and bridegroom, that is, a pair that must be strangers and wait for permission from society to become intimate. They must let the bonds of prejudice keep them from the full and free enjoyment of love, from genuinely human dealings with one another, and wait for the word of the priest, which would break these bonds, but only in order to be able to fasten them even more firmly. Each should feign a platonic abstinence toward the other, which is not in the nature of things, but lies in the barbarism of civilized society. Each should regard the other with a certain timidity and with an eye toward eternity. And once married, both will wonder how they could have been so blinded before. For what they receive will not correspond to their previous hopes. Before enthusiasm, now shallow ordinariness, before idealism, now often frightening experience. And none of this will have been or could have been anticipated by the bridal couple, because society refused to let them get to know one another better or look upon one another with understanding eyes. They will instead be chained together for life.

Yet, on rare occasions, the love of the bride may endure in marriage. But then, to whom is it entrusted to consecrate that love, and permit it to be full true love? The priest. So, society considers the love of one person to another, it considers this pure relationship between people, to be impure, and not strong enough to be recognized as valid for its own sake, without the intervention of the church. Do you hear, Marie, what the priest says to you? He explains that your previous love for Arthur was unholy and that only he, an agent of the church, can sanctify it. He explains to you that, in actuality, it is not good to marry, but that the church takes into account human weakness and consecrates marriage by putting its seal on it. He spurns your love, and claims that it only gets real power in front of the altar. He binds you to Arthur forever, and yet at the same time he impresses on you that the true marriage of the heart is to be made only with the bridegroom of heaven.

And you, Arthur, do you hear the words of the priest? He calls out all your past relationships as wicked, sins of the flesh, unworthy of God and man. He reviles your whole past life — and you are not contrite? Doesn't your soul cry out that it is unworthy of the sanctification of the church? You who stand here resolutely before the altar of the crucified God, who shall protect your marriage and be your advocate with the heavenly Father, you do not consider how often you have sinned against the holiness of that altar and the commandments of that crucified one? Get out! You enlist the help of the altar and do not believe in the power of its consecration. You appear before the Crucified, but you do not believe in him or in his words.

Marie! Arthur! No, you don't hear the priest. You consider this celebration in front of the altar a mere formality that is necessary, but that you would like to get over as quickly as possible, and the deeper meaning of which is lost to you, indeed to society as a whole. And yet you do not have the strength to shake off this form, which is now nothing more than an empty bondage.

That's our society. It still allows itself to be held by the ties that bind it to the church, but it no longer believes in this bond. Everything it does has been unchurched, and yet it does not have the strength to become a purely human, free society. Yes, this priest himself, is he still fully aware of what he is doing? I don't believe so. He considers his whole performance a formality — nothing more than his duty. Were he to apply all his sense to the task, society would decry him for being a fanatic and a darkling. This is Berlin. A belief that is feigned on the outside and violated inwardly at every moment. A society that is too weak to realize that it has actually already thrown off this belief, and too strong to once again allow itself to be completely bound by it.

Little Clare sat there for a long time, lost in thought. Only from time to time did she hear a few words from the priest, which branded her relationship with Arthur sinful, and which, as it were, banished her from society. For did not the priest think that the intercourse between man and woman was only right and sinless when given the consent of the church? The man and the woman are only pure if it is declared before the whole world that they possess no right of association in themselves or in their love, and that the church must first consecrate their relationship as a foreign power.

Little Clare only looked at the bridal couple closely when the priest came to the end of the ceremony, and they were about to exchange the rings. She knew it was Arthur. But it seemed impossible to her, it seemed too terrible a mockery that Arthur should deny her like this and join hands with another in an everlasting union. Her senses became confused. She was certain that, at any moment, Arthur would flee from the altar, fall at her feet, and beg her forgiveness for his treachery. And when the priest asked if he promised to belong to Marie forever, little Clare answered instead of him with a screaming, shrill "No!"

Marie was startled by the woman's voice, half mad, half despairing, protesting solemnly against the bond she was about to conclude. Suspicion began to grow in her heart, and she looked at Arthur with fearful, doubtful eyes. But her doubts vanished when she saw no unrest or embarrassment on his handsome face. Arthur turned around calmly and allayed the astonishment of the witnesses by remarking that it must be a mental patient who had been left unattended, and who needed their care.

The end of the story was that an unconscious pregnant woman was carried out of the church, after which the ceremony passed without further disturbance.

Had fate wanted to warn Marie? Was Marie's fate so favorable that it put stumbling block upon stumbling block in the way she trod so carelessly? It is possible. But Marie did not recognize this favor. She felt happy, and only foresaw a life of joy and contentment. Let's wish her a good night. May she revel in the sweet thought that she made the bond of love. May she not believe that she was dragged before an altar to become a wife who makes so and so many thalers in rents. May she believe that her father is happy today after getting a baron for a son-in-law. May she embrace the ideal of a pure and noble love of which she so often dreamed. May she think that Arthur would have loved her whether or not she had any money. May she be in Arthur's arms today, not out of a wife's duty, but in the fire of devotion. Who knows what tomorrow will bring. Maybe tomorrow her fantasies will fade when she comes to her senses after a night of intoxication. Perhaps tomorrow she will look at Arthur with colder and more understanding eyes. And if not tomorrow, the near future will surely reveal matters in the true light. Her ardor will perish at his coldness, her devotion will perish at his selfishness, a single remark from him will drive away all her idealistic fantasies. She will come to her senses and dealing with him will be a burden for her. She will want to push him away. But only now will she feel the tyranny of the church. What she abhors will be her duty. Society will demand of her that she keep the promise that she made before the altar today. And she would be disregarded if she did not respect her bondage.

Marie, with a self-mocking smile you'll think back to the conversation you had with Arthur that night.

"Arthur, I think the gods envied my good fortune when they allowed our marriage to be delayed twice today by such strange disturbances. Shouldn't I bring them a sacrifice to reconcile them?"

"Marie, sweet Marie, I know the sacrifice that shall keep all misfortune away from you."

"And that would be?"

"Sacrifice yourself to me, and I will always watch over you and keep you like a sanctuary."

"Yes Arthur, I know you will always love me. Do my feelings deceive me? Does my heart harbor only lies and false oracles? No, the voice inside me does not deceive. It calls out to me: Arthur will always be true to you."

"Certainly, Marie, that voice does not lie. And what a horrible person I would be if I wasn't touched by the tenderness and fire of your feelings. You noble soul, how could anyone knowingly deceive you? Yes, and if I had been false, would not your pure spirit purify me, would not just being near you make me better?"

"O Arthur!"

"O Marie!"

***

Little Clare woke up in a strange house. She felt miserable, defeated, and could hardly remember what had happened to her. Sometimes she imagined that it was she who had just been married, but then she recalled the true course of events and cried. She couldn't bear the looks of the people who stared at her as at a miraculous animal. When she felt a little stronger, she named the address of her apartment and asked for a ride home.

There she threw herself into the arms of her brother, who was only aroused to new fury by her story.

"That Arthur," he said, "is a lucky boy. He insults us and we have no means of revenge. We want to expose him in his wickedness, and we are taken for nonsensical liars and villains. We expose what he did, but he comes out purer and victorious. Chance leads you into the church when he is standing in front of the altar with his bride. None of this bothers him. And he doesn't use cunning or skill to free himself from the dangerous situations in which he finds himself. No. Only his selfishness and impudence save him. All misfortunes slip away, and because he presents fate with no weak spot where it could hit him, where it could cling to him, it must bounce off him powerlessly. He remains unharmed. He appears everywhere as the great, noble, levelheaded, misjudged, but brilliantly justified. Yes, such spirits are favored by circumstances. And I am supposed to swim with the current of ordinariness, I am supposed to throw myself at the feet of this baron and call out to him: Forgive me, noble, virtuous, ideal of society, that I have abused you, the gods will protect you. He would then pick me up and say: Stand up you weaker one, your mistakes are forgiven.

Let us become ordinary, little Clare, and society, which is now laughing at us, will be happy to welcome us back into its bosom. Let's get awfully vulgar, and believe me, we'll become as lucky as Arthur. Yes, we won't be able to get back at him if we don't become ordinary like him. Do you see little Clare, that is our society. You've just had your first look at it. The lie is protected, hypocrisy is rife, ordinariness rules, and whoever wants to be true, who foolishly believes that what is just will be recognized, that the human being will be respected, will be horribly disappointed. Let's work, little Clare, so that we can depend on this society as little as possible. Let us work, because soon there will be three of us."

Part Two

1. A Half Year Later

I see, my friend, that you have a somewhat dissatisfied expression on your face. Have I used too little romantic machinery for your taste? Is your pouting meant to force me to put a little more effort into romantic entanglements, to offer romantic shivers?

I know what you want! You want to see a deceived mother confronting the happy wife with her child in her arms and crying out: Behold the fruit of your husband's wickedness! You want to see Karl and Arthur in a dual — and to have Karl killed as well. You are curious as to whether, in our doubtful times, a father's curse is ineffective, or whether this curse will come true for Karl in one way or another. Up to now, Karl can still be called happy. He has suffered defeats, but he still stands tall and unbending. His solid principles make him proud and content. And little Clare, poor good little Clare, who was blessed by her father, is the only unfortunate one.

If you intend for it to go on like this, you say, it would be better to stop writing altogether! Shall Arthur never be reached by punishment? Why lead us around by the nose!

But I answer you that Arthur has been punished enough. What? Isn't life often a greater punishment than death? Especially the life that, with each new day, is already lost, lived in vain. But is it enough to say Arthur is punished by his insignificant life? He doesn't feel the punishment, you say. We want to see him suffer. Well, Arthur is married to Marie. Marie is married to Arthur. That is a penalty! Sheer punishment! Little Clare, on the other hand, may have been betrayed. But she remains free. And that is blessing enough!

But you are still not satisfied. Well, take heed. I will describe to you the fate of our friends, about half a year after the story we just told. Perhaps you will see the curse fulfilled, the punishment inflicted, and the blessing achieved.

Half a year later! Can you imagine all the experiences that our dear friends may have had over this long period of time?

Can you imagine how Marie felt when she first realized that she had been deceived? What changes might have taken place in her when she did not have "the sanctity of her feelings" respected in marriage?

Or did Arthur manage to maintain the illusion? Did he find it necessary to go to all the trouble for the sake of Marie's tranquility?

Did Karl accept the hard work that circumstances imposed on him without complaint? Or does he still prefer freedom to his daily bread?

And little Clare? Aren't you curious to see what happened to the pure, innocent, sorrowful mother? What feelings did she live with on the day that she was to give birth to the fruit of a frivolous betrayal?

You must see that I cannot answer all these questions in full. By skipping half a year, we must overlook much of the development of all these souls. And while I am once again rolling up the curtain for you, I will only be able to describe a few of the scenes.

2. The Married Couple

It is Sunday. The baroness must not have slept well, for her expression is sad and the melancholy features of her face seem to reveal a great emptiness. She looks straight ahead, almost thoughtlessly. Then the door opens, a man enters, and suddenly a certain liveliness pours over her face, a certain fire radiates from her eyes. But is it the fire of love that enlivens her gaze, is it the rays of joy that suddenly convey such vivacity to her countenance?

It is her husband who enters. Now we can explain the mocking expression that has settled around her mouth.

"Dear wife," the baron says, "won't you attend church with me today? Won't you turn back to the God whose service you have neglected for so long?"

How could that be Arthur, lustful, frivolous Arthur speaking? Arthur wants to go to church? Arthur has made himself a knight of God?

No, it's not Arthur, it's the Herr Baron. It's the husband who wants to go to church. It is the husband who has become pious. How he got there is a long story — the story of a six-month marriage.

Arthur had been very wrong to assume that he would soon be at peace with Marie.

At first Marie clung to him with a firm and heartfelt love. The strength of her passion inspired respect in him, and she subdued him without his realizing it. He sensed the strong spirit in Marie, which would never be content with a half-love, but which was also all-consuming in its devotion. He bent involuntarily, and so he was caught, he was dependent, before he could begin his cleverly devised operations.

But this dependence on a woman he didn't love was doubly annoying. Hadn't he married Marie for money? Didn't he want to continue his former happy life? Shouldn't Marie serve him only as an incidental means? And suddenly he has a woman who really wants to be a wife, who wants to see him as a real husband. This surprised him, his frivolity deserted him, and when he tried to pull himself up from the kind of stupor into which Marie's mighty mind had lowered him, it was too late.

He was a slave before he knew it, and in his effort to free himself, he piled clumsiness on top of clumsiness. Initially, he wanted to play the scoundrel, but it was no longer natural, it was awkward, without its former lighthearted charm.

And by opening Marie's eyes, it gave her the means to tame him and put him in his place. Marie could now rule over him in a new way. Whereas formerly it was through her passion, now it was through the guilt that she could instill in him with her quiet dignity.

His futile efforts made Arthur flat, unwilling, even weary of life. What could he hold on to, so as not to sink into nothingness in front of Marie? With what should he fill his empty soul, with what should he give it weight, so that it didn't appear hollow and unimportant to a woman?

Arthur had a certain desire for independence in himself. He felt that he was not destined to be an obedient husband, living the rest of his life under an oppressive and debilitating yoke. He didn't want to become completely insignificant — and so, he became pious.

Religion was the power by which he sought to give himself a certain dignity. When Marie reproached him for his meager love, he could reply in a self-satisfied manner that one ought to love only God in heaven. Instead of long, rational debates, in which Marie's sharp wit was sure to defeat him, he could quote a verse from the Bible. With a pious aphorism, he was able to avoid an argument and walk away the victor.

Now he was no longer the insignificant, subdued one. Now he could affect the demeanor of a conscientious pastor who wanted to lead a proud and free-spirited woman back to the love of God.

And dealing with him, which had previously been indifferent and boring for Marie, now became a prickly torment, a soul-destroying burden. How dreadful to have to endure daily the arrogance of a piety whose narrow views one has long since surpassed, and which one knows to have arisen only from the hollowness of the soul.

And Marie?

The insight into Arthur's character was a tremendous blow to her. She felt that this one pain that was tearing her soul apart must come to influence her whole life. Wasn't it a mockery of all that is called happiness in life, that she should be forever tied to this man, who was at first an insignificant slave, but now an intolerable preacher? This mockery made her own soul bitter, doubtful, frivolous. And just as she had to mock herself and her earlier delusion, so in the end life itself and all its contents became an object of mockery. If she was still allowed to move freely, was she allowed to cast off the oppressive yoke she had imposed on herself? No. And so, she had to seek her freedom in doubt, in ridicule.

And yet! Arthur was still interesting to her. It is true that she no longer clung to him with the interest of love, but he became necessary to her so that she might refresh her spirits in battle with him. Arthur became the embodied representative of the burden imposed on her by society's prejudices. So, he became part of her soul.

Hence that sudden light, that excitement in Marie's eyes as Arthur approached her. It wasn't the flash of hate, much less love. It was the liveliness of the magnetic pole as its opposite pole approaches.

Marie at first answered Arthur's question only with a mocking look, which her lively eyes cast inquisitively at the pious husband.

"How, my wife," continued Arthur in a measured tone, "how do you despise the church! You despise the holy power that bound us together and consecrated our relationship before God?"

This suggestion irked Marie. "You can't possibly imagine," she answered, "that the church has made itself dear and valuable to me in this way. You should be afraid to remind me of the indissolubility and so-called sanctity of a bond that can please neither you nor me."

This provided a good opportunity for Arthur to be unctuous. "You speak thus, O woman," he pronounced, "because your spirit is not humble. For my part, I do not grumble about what God has sent me and what the church has imposed on me, I bear and endure with a trusting heart, and I hope that one day you too will return to the love of God."

"Away with your humility," replied Marie. "My spirit is still calm enough to be contrite. Torment me no more, for you know your eloquence is wasted on me."

Arthur left, adopting a pitying expression. Oh, how unhappy, to have a wife who wants to be rational.

The brief conversation had upset Marie. She no longer sat rigid and gloomy as before but paced up and down the room. And yet she should have been used to these scenes. They had been repeating themselves regularly for some weeks. Piety, especially a moderate, calm one, like Arthur's was no reason for a divorce. The mental anguish that Marie had to endure could not justify dissolving a marriage. How wise, then, would have it been for Marie to bind her dull mind with the force of habit? Especially given that society demands every marriage, simply because it is a marriage, to be happy, or that one at least feigns happiness on the outside even if there is pain and suffering on the inside.

But Marie doesn't want this false veneer of peace. Arthur has no battles to endure because his paltry lack of complexity protects him from inner suffering. In his godly piety he stands completely pure before himself. Yes, he hopes for a blissful afterlife. And he will live a very calm and peaceful old age. Marie, however, whose spirit will not bend to the prescribed form, will not be crushed to the point of insensibility. Will she endure this fight long? I fear not for her. For fighting is the living element of a strong spirit.

3. Gustav

Strange thoughts went through Marie's mind when, soon after Arthur left for church, Gustav was announced. Gustav was the nephew of the privy councillor and he and Marie had been close friends in their youth. Later he went to a foreign university, where he stayed for two years. Gustav was dreamy by nature, childlike. He had always been attached to Marie with a passion the full strength of which he only discovered when he returned to find her married to Arthur. His devotion to Marie, instead of recoiling when he saw her in someone else's possession, came to life, and the trusting cousin became the reserved lover.

Marie had no affection for him. But was the glow that she saw in his eyes not more worthy of favor than Arthur's patronizing coldness? Didn't Gustav offer too good an opportunity to take revenge on Arthur for his heartless deceit?

Such thoughts momentarily whirled through Marie's head when she heard Gustav's name. But she did not love Gustav, and she was not yet so frivolous as to start a love affair with him out of mere mockery of the marital relationship, which made her unhappy. And yet, wasn't Gustav's fire dangerous to her? Didn't she have to worry that it might unexpectedly ignite her loveless spirit?

Marie struggled for a moment, then sent word back that she was unwell, and that Gustav could come back after Arthur had returned from church. She didn't want to be alone with Gustav so soon after that quarrel with her husband. And Gustav, who would not have let himself be turned away as a cousin, went away as a timid lover. He even wondered whether he might have aroused Marie's displeasure by being too obtrusively affectionate. Such innocence.

And now, when Marie knew that Gustav had gone away, she regretted having rejected him. She longed for a confidant to whom she could open her whole heart, to whom she could reveal all her suffering. Her pain was double agony because she had hidden it from the world until now. The good, innocent Gustav seemed to her the best confidant, but it is dangerous to confide in a lover.

Shouldn't Marie comfort Gustav, explain to him why she had turned him away? She had hardly made up her mind to let her relationship with Gustav cool off when she changed it again, sat down, and wrote the following letter:

My dear,

I know you love me, but when you read this letter, you must decide whether you believe it is conscionable to compound my misfortune of not being loved by one with the misfortune of being loved by another.

When I was engaged to Arthur, you were not here. So, you do not know the history of my marriage — what warnings fate sent my way and how blindly I rushed into my current unhappiness.

Yes, I am unhappy! You will be astonished. If you saw me with Arthur, you might have thought we were the happiest couple in the world. For both Arthur and I are forced to pretend for the sake of decency and lest we be laughed at for having a marriage that, in but its first few months, has already become alien and repugnant to us.

But on the inside, no two people could be less compatible than Arthur and I. Oh my friend, I am so open with you. You are the first and only one to whom I will empty my heart. Please do not take my frankness amiss. My heart is about to burst, it longs for a confidant, and I choose you because I know that you will not betray my trust.

You know my father. He knows nothing of life and the more intimate movements of the soul. I find no comforter in him.

So, listen to the story of my misfortune. When Arthur first approached me, oh what an ideal of nobility and manliness he was. What great thoughts did not swell his lips. How well he knew how to insinuate himself and present himself, as it were, as a higher, extraordinary being.

At least that is how I saw him. I used to have a boyfriend whom you never met. He was good but not graceful. The grace, the elegance in Arthur captivated me, and from his outward appearance I drew too hasty a conclusion as to his inwardness.

But after our marriage, the flow of his speech was suddenly lost. When I tried to talk to him rationally, with what trivialities did he mock my words!

I got to know him as selfish, and I did not hesitate to let him know. The demand I made for a certain sovereignty of soul perhaps offended him. In short, we became strangers to each other. And now, we are even more so.

But my zest for life is gone. I had with all the power of my mind been so attached to Arthur that, as that love waned from my heart, the free dynamism of my spirit and the energy of my sensibility were snatched away from my soul.

My living courage has withered. I feel that doubts, indeed, a certain indifference have taken hold of me, so much so that I have become incapable of soulful relations. The shameful confinement in which I now live swallows my feelings. I can no longer glow for anyone.

So, your love, oh Gustav, would always be a torment for me too, because it would always be hopeless. Better for you to be my friend, my confidant. Prove to me that there are still men who can live without placing selfish demands on another.

And I must reveal one last thing that is bothering me, and that is the main reason why I am writing to you now. That ungraceful friend, who must have known Arthur better, tried to dissuade me from the marriage by a peculiar means on the day of my wedding. The matter is too complex, so I will have to tell you in person. But at the time he seemed horrible to me, and now I see him in a different light.

I have not seen my friend since that day, and I don't know what became of him. But if you come to me, I want to tell you who he is and why I desire to know more about him now.

Come back soon, Gustav. I turned you away today because, in my current desperate state, and with my present distrust of humanity, which is only too well justified, I myself do not know what harsh and repellent actions I am committing.

Come to me soon, but come as a friend, not as a lover. Come as a friend with whom I can express such harsh and reproachful remarks against my husband, because he will not misuse them and because he must know my heart. Do not come as a lover who would only too readily take advantage of my dislike of Arthur.

When Marie wrote this letter, she didn't give much thought to whether she would send it or not. Did she perhaps suspect that it might bring about a change in her fate — that her heart, empty of love, might at last have found a man whose friendship could lift it up again and free it from the torment of abandonment?

Now that Gustav was aware of Arthur's character, was it not possible that, upon meeting Karl, he could bring out the truth of his accusation against Arthur, at which everyone had previously scoffed?

Be careful, Herr Baron. A storm is brewing just over your head. Perhaps tomorrow you will already have been unmasked.

Marie gave her letter to her maid, so that it would reach Gustav safely.

* * *

"A letter, Herr Baron," the girl said to Arthur when he returned from church.

"A letter," Arthur replied. "To who?"

"To Herr Gustav."

"Well, you don't need to bother me with it any further. I'm sure it is innocent. What more can it be than an invitation to lunch. Go ahead and deliver it straightaway."

"Herr Gustav was here in the morning, Madame didn't let him in, and immediately afterward she wrote this letter and told me to be certain that it is placed in Herr Gustav's hands."

"That's fine, you can go now."

The maid departed.

"But wait a moment," Arthur thought to himself. "Haven't I noticed Gustav taking an interest in my wife?"

He called the girl back.

"Show it to me," he said. "It doesn't appear to be short. I wonder what secrets my wife has with Gustav. If it contains nothing offensive, Gustav will receive it soon enough."

Arthur read it.

"Aha," he said to himself, "they want to expose me. They hate and mistrust me. I must try to prevent them. Marie is still thinking of Karl, and eventually she will send her confidant Gustav to him. The solution is to anticipate that in advance. We ourselves will bring Gustav together with Karl. Gustav doesn't know him, only what might be revealed through him. Well, isn't it the surest proof of our innocence that we didn't hesitate to send Gustav to Karl? At least we can manage it in such a way that we appear most generous. What next? Little Clare is still beautiful, and Gustav is receptive to beauty. Who knows, this might rid us of this dangerous family friend. Either way, I'm going to run into Karl again sooner or later. If that happens unexpectedly, it could be dangerous for me. So, let's hold the reins in our hands and lead this thing ourselves. Gustav can even serve as my spy."

Arthur had not become so pious as to lose his former cunning. He knew that Karl could harm him one way or another. That's why he never lost sight of him. He also feared his wife would resume her correspondence with him, and that is why he had the maid inform him about all her letters.

His plan was soon arranged.

When Gustav returned as Marie had instructed, Arthur intercepted him without informing Marie of his presence.

"Dear Gustav," said Arthur, "I know you are a sensitive person. I know that you take pleasure in doing good. At church today, the preacher was able so vividly to describe to us the plight of the poor, these beloved children of Christ, that I am now determined to carry out an intention that I have repeatedly neglected out of other considerations. Would you like to assist me in doing this good work, dear Gustav?"

Gustav, childlike and inexperienced, always had a certain respect for Arthur. And this seemed to him the very essence of Christian love and gentleness. How unchristian would it be to say no to a proposal that was so beautifully formulated?

He replied from the bottom of his heart.

"Well then, dear Gustav, I know a poor brother and sister here in Berlin who live in the most miserable circumstances. I have chosen you to bring joy and contentment back to the poor. I will tell you where they live. Visit them and find a pretext to give them money."

"But Herr Baron, why would you deprive yourself the joy of seeing the fruits of your good deeds?"

"You must know, dear Gustav, one of the two siblings is a beautiful girl who came to see me a few weeks ago. In short, my wife is jealous, and it probably doesn't suit a husband to associate with a fallen woman. Besides, I'm too humble to allow myself to be honored, even if it were as a benefactor. I like to do good, but I don't like to hear thanks for it."

"I admire you, Herr Baron."

"Leave it, leave it, Herr Gustav. And one more thing. That girl's brother does not believe in God. Therefore, I have specifically sought him out, to see whether bestowing a great gift on him might lead him back to God."

"I will immediately get to work putting your plan into action."

"Very good, I like that. But I must remind you of one thing: Please do not tell them who the gift came from because, as I said, I do not like receiving thanks that belong only to God. He gave me wealth to use wisely."

What a noble and great soul, Gustav thought as he left the baron. Pure virtue, the disinterested love of humanity, is already evident in Arthur's face. How happy my cousin must be with him! And I wanted to tarnish this pure, beautiful marital relationship, no, I have already tarnished it with my selfish love for

Marie! I wanted to deceive this noble man. Shame on you Gustav! From now on I will think of Marie no more.

* * *

"You must, dear wife, take better care with your maid. I found a letter that she must have carelessly dropped. I opened it to see if I might be able to deliver it quicker in person."

With these words, Arthur returned to Marie her letter to Gustav. His calm demeanor outraged her even more than if he had flared up in anger.

Seeing her plan with Gustav and Karl betrayed, Marie had to give up thinking of Gustav any longer as a confidant and a messenger for Karl.

4. The Siblings

There are, in Berlin, narrow alleys barely wide enough to walk through. If you wish to keep your boots clean, there is no way to navigate them safely. In the middle of each, there is a gutter, which spreads filth and stench far and wide. Here is where the poor artisans live, whom you will recognize instantly by their sallow and indifferent faces.

Do you know faces? Oh, look around you attentively, appreciate the face of your neighbor, consider it closely and read out the spirit there. Don't walk the streets carelessly and thoughtlessly. Look around you and, often enough, you will be able to see the spiritual physiognomy of a city, of a people, in the faces you encounter.

In the way men behave publicly in the light of day you will find their character most faithfully drawn. Come with me: If you only meet stooped, uncertain figures, if you see no eye shining with a cheerful, open meaning, if you see only pressed, low foreheads closed to all free and universal interests, if the only ones who walk proudly are the gendarmes, then you know that these people have had every sense of freedom suppressed, that they have no notion of a public life, that the particular and ordinary affairs on their mind amount to dull selfishness. A free man, on the other hand, also walks about freely and cheerfully. And one can read from his face the share he has among his equals, the share he has in humanity.

Now, among this indifferent, scurrying crowd, look at those pale, sickly faces around which poverty has wound a crown of thorns. One reads in them the fear for their daily bread. The stooped figure is like a question mark that rises up to the sky to ask why one exists if one only ever knows pressure and distress.

Such people live in those alleys — people who, from one day to the next, eke out a meager existence through the labor of their hands. Come up with me to a poor shoemaker's house. It's the middle of summer, and you will find him in his musty room surrounded by a smell that would make you ill were you to live in it for a single hour. To cook his food, he must keep his oven burning amid the summer heat. And despite the discomfort of his apartment, what is the first thing he thinks of when he receives a few pennies for an expertly healed boot? Will he earn enough to pay the rent.

And this man is fortunate. He has two rooms. But he can't afford the rent on such a palace, so he gave the second room to a poor brother and sister. Let's take a closer look at this room as well. Here you find a pair of beds, shabby and unclean, a pair of wooden stools, a broken table, a desk, a pair of books, and some children's clothes drying by the window — a veritable mess of random things.

At the window there is a girl trying in vain to sew, for the young child she has on her lap is restless and screaming, probably from hunger. The girl is pale and haggard and must have been ill for a long time. And yet you will recognize a trace of majesty and pride in her still beautiful face.

The girl is little Clare. The upheavals she has experienced in such a short space of time, the sufferings, which formed such a terrible contrast to her earlier peaceful life, have left her ill. After this first pain, did her soul wish to escape a life that offered only bitter and dreary experiences?

Karl could not work much during little Clare's illness. Caring for her devoured his time, and she was destitute and without prospects. The day little Clare was to give birth drew closer and closer, representing new forms of need and deprivation. And so, they finally had to move into this apartment.

He had not yet succumbed completely, but his spirit had lost its vitality and freshness. A certain discontent, less with himself than with his circumstances, humiliated him and made him self-conscious. He no longer approached society with a dominating pride. He became angry. And a prickly resentment took the place of his earlier contempt.

But resentment makes the spirit unfree. It is not a mood in which a spirit can create. Thus, Karl had turned from a journalist to a copyist. He wrote and corrected sheets for a tiny wage.

The day that the ailing little Clare lay in childbirth in that cramped room was a terrible one. The young newborn screamed and howled, as if protesting against the misery and tribulation that awaited him.

At the same time, Karl performed his clerical work with perpetual anxiety about the future, without rest, without a break. Didn't Karl have to regard any time he allowed himself to rest as a theft he was committing against the welfare of his sister and her child? Wouldn't he fear a whole day of misery and scarcity for every hour he spent away from his work?

And always having to look back at the shamefulness that brought him into such a position. Truly, it takes an unusual humility or an unusually strong self-consciousness not to succumb to such torment.

Fundamentally, however, Karl was a very strong spirit. He was irascible. But he was able to remain firm so long as things did not look too bad on the outside.

And yet, won't the misery gnawing at his soul dull him, won't the intractability of his circumstances, which he had previously considered unimportant, force him to come to peace with them? Won't constant worry about his daily bread eventually produce in him an indifference as to how he acquires it?

It is evening. Karl has gone out to collect payment for some corrections he has done. Little Clare anxiously awaits him. She and her child are starving because there is not a penny left in the house. Finally, Karl returns.

"Oh, it's disgraceful," he exclaims. "One must fall at these people's feet, one must beg them on one's knees, to get what one has earned. Then the man wanted to make deductions, because he knows that I am poor and need the money. I answered him seriously and appealed to his conscience. I pointed to the injustice of his offer. But he then became coarse. He was surprised that a poor devil like me should dare to reason and not humbly accept what is offered. When I persisted with my request, he finally said that he could no longer agree to payment today, and that I should come back tomorrow. What does he care if three people go hungry? I despised him too much to beg him, and here I am without money. Oh, the misery of being dependent on such people."

Little Clare nodded her head and said nothing. When you are poor you learn resignation.

And you will go to bed hungry today.

5. August the Shoemaker

Karl had sat down morosely in a corner when his roommate Herr August the shoemaker entered. Herr August was far from handsome. The constant crouching on the stool had made his form crooked. But you would have fallen in love with him if you had seen the expression of joy and affection that transfigured his face when little Clare returned his greeting in a friendly manner. This love, which expressed itself in his face, was beautiful and pure. It was the compassionate love of misery for misery. Poverty makes us all equal, and only like can love like. When a rich person is attracted to a poor one, there is still a certain elevation, a proud condescension, in their love. Similarly, a kind of humility and dependence will always be mingled with the love of the poor for the rich.

But the love of misery for misery is pure and disinterested. It is the human's love for the human without any extrinsic consideration. It is the only consolation of the poor.

When little Clare first moved into the apartment, it seemed to August as if the sun, which otherwise never shone into his stuffy room, had illuminated his poor home with its rays. The simple dignity, the calm nobility, with which little Clare bore her misery reconciled him with his own. It was the first time he had ever seen a strong human being. And this sight ennobled him.

His silent admiration for little Clare had an invigorating effect on him. He now worked with less unhappiness. He had found some comfort and solace.

This is Herr August, as he entered:

"So sad, Karl," he said. "I myself have opportunity and reason enough to be disappointed. But for some reason, the misery doesn't really stay with me anymore. Well, tomorrow is the first, I'm supposed to pay the rent, and I don't know how I will. Our landlady is far too clever to offer us a lease for a quarter of the year. We must pay monthly, so we have a nice, daily reminder to put something away for her. Now tomorrow is payment day and I have nothing. You probably don't have anything either, so we'll be thrown out of the house. But it doesn't matter. We'll stick together, right?"

"Move out immediately?" Karl said. "But can't the landlord wait a couple of days? That doesn't require too much compassion."

"Well, you don't know our Berlin landlords, Herr Karl. They know all too well that if they wait and let the rent accumulate, they'll end up with nothing. I have experience. We will have to go and someone else will be brought in who might pay more regularly at first. The landlords want their money. Ours has several houses here in Berlin, but the more they have, the more hard-hearted they become. Compassion! Well, for the landlord we are just tenants whose purpose is to ensure that his house does not stand empty without paying interest. He throws the tenant out of the house, not the man. And if the tenant cannot find a new place, that does not concern him."

"A beautiful philosophy," replied Karl.

"You see, Herr Karl, everyone has their own philosophy, and I have mine too. Yes, I have had different philosophies in my life. Let me tell you my story for a change." August sat down. "While it is not very interesting, it is good enough to put tiresome thoughts of money and the rent out of our heads.

"I prefer to ignore my memories of the beatings I received from my master. When I was an apprentice, my whole philosophy was speculation — for a tip, or for a ham sandwich that a cook slipped me here or there.

"Then I became a journeyman and fell in love with a girl who sold flowers. My philosophy then became going to dance halls and singing lewd love songs. I was cheerful and happy and already planning to marry my beauty when she was seduced by a rich gentleman, leaving me stranded.

"Then I had a completely different philosophy. I gave myself over to drinking schnapps and became a rather wild fellow. I drank brandy almost out of revenge against my lot, which I wanted to forget. I didn't want to care about the world anymore, now that my only joy had been destroyed.

"Then I heard from my buddies that a man had appeared here in Berlin who wanted to establish a temperance club.[1] He gave public lectures and had no greater ambition than to ban all schnapps-drinking people from Berlin.

"This man annoyed us. We thought he had no respect for us and wanted to abuse us. So, he had to be punished. It's easy for him to talk, we said. He'll have his wine every day but wants to deprive us of our only consolation. He should improve our situation first and then drinking schnapps will take care of itself.

"And look, Herr Karl, that's still my opinion, even though I don't drink brandy anymore. The rich would like to blame us poor for our declining condition. But they will never consider that it is they themselves who are holding us down by their mere existence. They press on us and then when we feel pressed and satisfy our urge for spirit with spirits, they revile us. But they are ashamed if they pay us no notice, and they condescendingly feel that we have a right to their consideration. So, then what do they do? They offer us benevolent teachings and preach morality. They feign to educate us instead of allowing us the means and the time to educate ourselves. They try to fob us off with words and think they have done everything possible by superficially asking us to give up drinking. But you can see for yourself how difficult it is to let go of a passion. They can't even sacrifice their passion for possessing, and I honestly believe that the poor man's propensity to drink is even stronger than the rich man's propensity to possess. Drinking, intoxication, is the only way poor people momentarily free themselves from the torment of their lives.

"But I get ahead of myself. What I was just discussing is part of my current philosophy. But first I should tell you how I came to this philosophy.

"So, the temperance man annoyed us, and we decided to taunt him.

"One Sunday we went to his lecture quite drunk. We took bottles of brandy with us and drank them in front of him. His followers got angry and wanted to throw us out, but he would not allow it. Instead, he calmly asked us to come closer so that we could understand him better. My friends were taken aback by this and left, but I was on a mission and wanted to prove to him that, for a real drinker, what he said was useless.

"But I had placed too much faith in my stubbornness. The man knew how to appeal to my conscience. I became aware of myself. I was genuinely ashamed and could not seem to suppress the feeling with more drinking. In the end, I left the meeting with the chairman, and left the brandy behind.

"Now I became a thinker. I reflected on my situation, which I had previously tried to forget. And so, a different philosophy took shape within me.

"I asked myself whether drinking was the only means by which man suppressed his consciousness. And do you know how I answered this question?

"Most people do not only get drunk on brandy and spirited drinks. Most of them live their lives in a certain state of intoxication.

"Some get drunk on money. And money intoxication also takes away our respect for ourselves and for others. Just like brandy intoxication, it fills us with animal desires and animal indifference to everything noble. In addition, the brandy drinker has many bright moments while the money man has almost none. The drunk might commit murder once in a moment of unconsciousness. The money man commits one at every moment. He murders the souls of the poor whom he oppresses and who, as a result of their poverty, cannot develop as human beings. Just one rich person sacrifices the education and freedom of countless poor people.

"Another will intoxicate himself with power. In his drunken power he believes that the world revolves around him. Everything exists for his sake, and he will strike down anyone who tries to oppose him. He too murders a thousand souls. Jealous of his reputation, he does not let others speak for fear they might say something detrimental to his superiority. To nourish his power, he withers the existence of everyone else. He refuses to rein in his arbitrariness. He wants to make the rest of us slaves, to rob us of our freedom. Intoxication with power is therefore just as immoral, indeed even more immoral, than intoxication with money or brandy. He too stifles the consciousness of being human; he too destroys respect for man and his rights.

"Still others are intoxicated by religion. They want to glorify heaven and forget the earth. But they also want to thunder down everything that does not conform with their views. Such intoxication is more dangerous than immoral and more inhuman than dangerous.

"And others get intoxicated with love or with prejudices, yes, there are even those who get intoxicated with their own unique and original passion. I knew someone who cared only about his kitten [*Kätzchen*], who only lived for his cat. So, he had — pardon the expression, little Clare — a hangover [*katzenjammer*] at the same time as his intoxication.[2]

"Thus, I came to see nothing in the world, nothing but intoxication. Everything seemed unreasonable and drunk to me now. Everything like an eternal and insatiable frenzy. The sun, moon, and earth turned around in my brain and I became intoxicated with the thought of the intoxication of the world.

"But my philosophy would not have been complete if I had not included myself and made my own intoxication the object of my reflection.

"One shouldn't get drunk on one's philosophy, I thought. One must also be conscious of one's own thoughts, and out of this philosophy about my philosophy my newest and current philosophy arose.

"You must not, I reasoned, intoxicate yourself on the thought of intoxication. You must at least find something to hold on to, otherwise you will stumble around ridiculously. I looked for a solid pillar but couldn't find one anywhere. Justice, I said, is also twisted and unstable. We must work and have nothing. Is that justice? Others do nothing and have everything. Is that justice? Reason is made dizzy and uncertain by obscurantists. Those who don't think are lifted to the top, and those who do think sink. How is that reasonable? So, you have nothing to hold on to but yourself!

"You must educate yourself through thinking, and in the end, you will become firm in yourself and no longer waver from one affliction to another.

"But how will the general intoxication, in which people have always been entangled, come to an end, that's what I'm wondering, Herr Karl.

"When we poor people, who have been prevented from thinking, begin to know ourselves as something, when we gradually become aware of what right and what reason lie dormant in us, then perhaps we too will one day become public, and give practical lectures on the money intoxication, the power intoxication, and the prejudice intoxication. We will know how to tame those drunken brutes. We will be people who hold on to themselves.

"Up to now, of course, we poor people have been much more caught up in the frenzy of prejudice than in the frenzy of brandy. Against the former, however, no temperance clubs are likely to be permitted.

"No harm. Perhaps we will come to temper ourselves. And we will be all the more ashamed of our intoxication and seek to erase it."

"You are a man," Karl said, "worthy of working alongside Jakob Böhme and Hans Sachs.[3] But all this philosophy does not get us a penny for tomorrow's rent."

"That doesn't do any harm either," replied our wise Herr August. "We still live in the time of intoxication and chance, so you can never determine in advance what may happen tomorrow. Bright flashes can occur. Our landlord, for example, could have a moment of lucidity when his dizziness leaves him, when he feels like a human being. He then may show us some leniency. Or some traveling man has a human moment, comes to me tomorrow and pays me for a pair of boots in advance. Or, or . . . what do I know? In the frenzy of our times, things can twist and turn in unexpected ways."

"So, your whole philosophy," Karl observed, "boils down to waiting."

"Yes, Herr Karl, we'll wait, but let's be vigilant. They think nothing of us. We ourselves have nothing. But it is possible that the future is ours. So, let's wait, Herr Karl, let's wait."

And with this consolation in their hearts, they went to bed with nothing in their stomachs.

6. Nobility

"You genuinely seem to belong to the temperance club. But the world is so twisted that, if they learned how you were acting, they would say: That man is not right in his head."

With these words, August expressed his gratitude toward Gustav, who, as luck would have it, began the mission that Arthur had given him on that fateful first of the month.

Introducing himself to August as an earlier acquaintance of Karl's, he inquired about his circumstances. He pretended to be shocked by August's description of Karl's situation, and, feigning a moment of charitable outburst, paid their rent. "He'll know how to make up for it over time," he said.

But he had become curious about the unhappy mother, whom August ardently portrayed as so beautiful, so good, so patient. Did he perhaps suspect that here in this narrow alley he would find a pure, genuine woman who would make up for his hopeless love for Marie? Gustav was a dreamer. He believed that he must one day see his ideals embodied before him. And it seemed to him as if he might find the perfect, true woman here wrapped in the ragged cloaks of poverty, living in painful penance for a crime that was not her own.

In short, he no longer wanted to content himself with the role of a benefactor from afar. He wanted to see his offspring for himself. But how should he introduce himself to them? He needed Herr August. But would August agree with his plan? Would he not become suspicious?

He confessed to August that he did not know Karl previously. He had, he said, resolved to support Karl out of sheer charitable impulses, which he could easily satisfy because of his wealth. This wouldn't be the only time he would come to inquire about Karl's circumstances, he explained, as he'd like to help. Only he would leave it to Mr. August to invent the pretexts under which he would receive the gifts.

August was shocked by this generosity. Either the man is very sober, he thought, or he's drunk on charity.

"But now," Gustav continued, "I would like to get to know Herr Karl myself. I fear that if I come to him as a rich, distinguished man, he will not receive me well, or be inclined to become my friend."

"You're quite right about that," August replied. "Ever since Herr Karl has become destitute, he has developed great anger toward all noble people. If you offered him money, he would throw you out the door. But if you said you were coming without any secondary intentions, he would not trust you or allow you to visit again."

"Then how about you introduce me to the siblings as a simple journeyman shoemaker? Herr Karl must have a fondness for shoemakers if only because of you."

After some back-and-forth, August agreed to the suggestion. He didn't want to deprive his friend Karl of such a benevolent benefactor.

So, Gustav came back in the evening as a shoemaker and took part in Herr August's philosophical investigations quite naturally and without suspicion.

The sight of little Clare did not make a strong impression on him. A mother of flesh and bones with a child of flesh and bones looks very different from the virgin messiah mother in a painting by Raphael. If the painter had the tones of a child's voice at his command in addition to those of his color, we would often enough run away from his picture instead of standing in front of it admiringly.

Gustav, the romantic, the dreamer, had imagined our little Clare quite differently. The busy commotion of a mother who is occupied with her child, now laying out the laundry, now breastfeeding, now singing and swinging back and forth, was bound to repulse rather than attract a rapturous and sensitive mind like Gustav's. He had imagined a young mother there, gazing at the pious, gentle child on her lap with tender affection. Reality — turbulent, active reality — offended him.

Thus, Gustav's first visit to Karl gave him little satisfaction. Oh, the innocent ones who, like all sentimental spirits, want to find romance and comfort even in poverty.

Nevertheless, the novelty of the relationship into which he had gotten himself led him back to the brother and sister the next day. And soon his evening visits became a habit.

Because, over time, little Clare started to interest him. The weakness from her previous illness and her confinement gradually dissipated. Her beauty developed more and more victoriously and conquered the withered morbidity of her body. She no longer had to occupy herself so much with her child, she could join in the conversation. And the peculiar freedom of her views surprised Gustav.

Gustav was almost never alone with the siblings. He would visit them in the evenings when he could slink through the streets in his journeyman's coat. Then at twilight August always had time to chat for an hour. That's why Gustav had never heard the story of little Clare's earlier circumstances. And he had no idea that he was related to the child whose cries often irritated him. He noticed that Karl had more talent than a mere scribe, and he was curious, but he thought it improper to let his curiosity show.

He also took less interest in Karl. He was a little repelled by the somber, unfriendly way in which he endured his fate. Much more did he admire little Clare's calm and quiet majesty. He wished to be able to improve their situation in a permanent and thorough manner. He made plans, and since he had become so occupied with little Clare at heart, he resolved to show her his affection externally as well.

But little Clare paid no attention. Her mind was too mature to embark again in the dalliance of love. She noticed Gustav's affection but hoped that her indifference would cure the journeyman shoemaker of his quiet romanticism.

"If only I were rich," Gustav declared one evening. "How I long to lighten your sad lot. I would use all my possessions to make you happy."

"Don't believe that," Karl sniffed. "If you were rich you wouldn't think of us at all."

"And even if you were thinking of us," added little Clare, "I don't think I would accept your kindness. I would be suspicious of your sensitive heart. I would foist selfish thoughts on you. The distance between us would always keep us apart. In short, I would prefer poverty to dependence on a rich man."

"Well said," August concluded.

Little Clare's pride only stimulated our Gustav even more. But why was he so worried about her fate? Did he truly love her, as he told himself?

No, he merely clung to her with the interest of a romantic who has finally found someone who could disrupt his monotony and boredom like a character in a novel. Making little Clare happy was more of a fantastic caprice on his part than the result of any goodness of heart. But that only made him struggle with his plans all the more. He wanted to pull little Clare up to him. He no longer wanted to pretend to be the shoemaker's journeyman in front of her. He wanted to show her his true form and to surprise her with the realization that a noble person could love without interest. He wanted . . . Yes, he wanted everything! But his intentions were far too romantic to find any starting point in reality.

He asked Arthur for advice.

"You won't be able to help the girl, dear Gustav," Arthur said, "if you don't help her brother at the same time."

"But how?"

"Karl," Arthur replied, "was a journalist. He's talented, he'd do a pretty good job as a secretary in an office."

"You give me an excellent idea. My father has authority at the ministry. I know there is a position open for a man to oversee the magazines, to rectify the lies and distortions of the bad press. How about we see if Herr Karl can take the job?"

"Do that, do that, and the good Lord will reward you for helping two poor people."

Arthur will intercede for Karl? But Arthur wants to avoid being in contact with Karl and little Clare again? How does that rhyme?

Listen to Arthur's reflections and you will be able to understand his behavior.

"It's all going better than I could have hoped. My peace and contentment will soon be complete.

"Yes, we are all sinful people, and soon there will be no one left who can stand before me and brag: Lo and behold, I'm better than you. Soon I shall be justified before myself, and even God, I hope, will look upon me with merciful eyes.

"That Karl was always a thorn in my side. It annoyed me that he wanted to be better than other people. Sometimes it enraged me to think that this Karl wanted to keep himself proud and pure. But now, who knows what he'll settle for! And so long as he stays away, so long as he lies lurking in that alley, like a hungry wolf, I still have a certain fear and respect for him. I always worry that he could still be dangerous to me, that he could break out of his hiding place one day, bringing disaster. But once we have him tied to a job and his daily bread, then we can talk sensibly to him. He will become ordinary and conform to our order.

"And this Gustav, the pure dear innocent one who was always so admired and indulged. At ground, he's just selfish.

"And if little Clare gets involved with him? Well, all the better for me. Then she becomes a girl like any other. And if Marie also discovers the nature of my relationship with her, would she be able to make a great crime out of it?

"But what does Marie actually want? She can no longer pretend to be high-and-mighty with me! No, she must bow to me now that I've found out what she was planning with Gustav.

"Yes, yes, we are all weak, sinful people. And soon no one will be able to come to me and say: Lo and behold, I am better than you.

"Yes, my happiness will soon be complete, my peace no longer disturbed."

* * *

Once Gustav had formed his plan, he could not rest until he had carried it out. He immediately spoke to his father before even asking Karl, because he thought Karl would have to grab the opportunity with both hands. His father agreed to everything.

Gustav now wanted to reveal to Karl his true status, and what a beautiful and secure position he had arranged for him. He thought of bringing him the news personally, but he also wanted to surprise little Clare in the right circumstances and decided that she should not find out who he was for the time being. He would leave for a while, and only once Karl had settled into his new position would he come back and reveal his true form to little Clare. Behold the wealthy one, who took pains to improve the lot of the poor.

Oh! Nobility beyond nobility!

When Gustav surprised Karl with his proposal, Karl felt even more defeated. This was the last and extreme humiliation, which threw him completely to the ground. He was humbled by the desolation of his condition, in which one could offer him such a thing without blushing. And he had become so weak that he could no longer dismiss Gustav's proposal on the spot with contempt — he struggled.

7. The Father's Curse

"I'm tired, little Clare, of struggling with the world, and yet I'm ashamed that I'm tired. But I see that this world, this unreasonableness that exists, cannot be fought. If we want to be independent, it takes revenge on us and casts us out. It crushes us, it doesn't recognize us as full-fledged combatants. I have only contempt for this world, but it wants me to give up and let it feed me.

"I am weary, little Clare, and because I am weary, I can no longer benefit from reason. Weary people belong to this weary and limp society. That is why it weakens us through deprivation and misery. Our spirit must become ordinary, and then society welcomes us with joy. And now that I am too emaciated to be a free man, it is best that I allow myself to be directed by this society — make myself comfortable with its prejudices, exploit its conditions for your benefit and mine, and drag along my miserable life in a useless baggage train.

"Believe me, my sister, it is a terrible mockery of myself and of society that tears my soul apart as I conform to society and make a truce with it.

"Only the despair of myself and the victory of reason drives me to this unnerving ordinariness. And yet I feel it. It is neither right nor true, this despair. I feel it is my own weakness alone that gives me that doubt. But a weak, doubting man is no longer suitable as a warrior of reason.

"I will celebrate my own funeral without hope of rebirth if I accept Gustav's offer. And yet I am not determined enough to wrap myself in the shroud of poverty, or to prefer a real, actual death to this death of the spirit.

"Yes, little Clare, though I am now close to suffering my defeat, yet I am a martyr of liberty. Every stroke of the pen shall wound and harm me more than an arrow penetrating a Christian saint. I will become a living sacrifice offered with its bitter smell to the Moloch of condemnation and social bondage.

"Every word that I will write will be one more thorn in the crown that the sneering servants of the existing state of affairs want to put on my forehead, which I previously displayed so high and freely.

"But I'm starving, little Clare, you're starving, and the child is starving. Hunger, king of the poor, I bow to you. You have achieved what society could not achieve without you. You have dulled my spirit, killed my independent sense, and made me a servant of the police. I accept the job.

"And you see, little Clare, we will live quite well and comfortably, from now on we will lack for nothing. And since we suddenly have something to eat again, society will respect us again.

"We will be able to dress well again, and if we are properly dressed, society will honor us. We will be wealthy, and people will visit us and accept visits from us. We will revel in the gossip of the day. We will concern ourselves with every detail of our neighbors' life. In short, we will be good, dear, ordinary people. And I will have a job.

"Little by little, perhaps our memories of what we used to be and what we used to think will fade. We will feel comfortable. We will live gentle lives. We may even get married. Yes, because I have a job, I will also get a wife.

"Finally, we will die, and our deaths will be just as ordinary as our lives. And we will be buried, and people will say: It is a shame, but dying is human. Gently may their ashes rest.

"And society will wish for many subjects just like us.

"Tomorrow, little Clare, we'll have something to eat. I will accept the job."

And with that, the curse of the father was fulfilled.

8. Little Clare to Karl

My brother, I have left you and will not return.

If you listen to me carefully and have respect for me, you will leave me where I am and not demand that I come back. You will not force me to lead a life that I will always be tempted willfully to abandon.

I don't think you were knowingly trying to deceive me. On the contrary, I see quite well that your constant preoccupation with yourself and your own grief has not allowed you to consider me or inquire as to what I might say about our new situation.

By chance I found out that the man who introduced himself to us as a poor journeyman shoemaker is the one who got you your job. This man's name is Gustav. He is the son of the councillor you work for. And he is related to Arthur and his wife.

Even when he was pretending to be a journeyman shoemaker, Gustav made no secret of his interest in me. I must assume that he's taken us under his wing for the same reason. I hear he'll return from his trip soon, so I left you today.

I'm not about to make myself the plaything of childish love again. I'd rather starve than be tormented and dependent. I want nothing to do with these noble people who are without spirit and see every relationship as nothing more than a means for alleviating their boredom. For that I am too proud.

But that wouldn't have been enough to drive me out of your house. For if I remained with you, wouldn't I be in constant fear of running into Arthur or even coming into contact with his wife? With all my pride, and though I am long beyond thinking only of Arthur and his treachery, such an encounter would be painful to me.

Do you think we women have no feelings? Do you think we don't also have the need for freedom and self-determination? Do you think we must take everything as you please and as you arrange it?

No, as I said, I prefer independent deprivation to that depressed and eternally anxious state in which I would have to live with you.

And where am I now? I am with August, who especially helped me on Gustav's trail. I will stay with him. I will help him endure his poverty. I will run his small business for him and despite all the hardships I will at least be at peace.

Perhaps I know August's noble disposition better than you. I recognized it while we stayed with him and found a strength in him that I admired often enough. Certainly, if I were to marry a man, it would be August.

With this simple and strong mind, I shall one day live a more significant and satisfied life than I would in your boring and spiritless societies. August is a person who also knows what being a human means. He knows best how to treat and respect another without obtrusive misery, without constant preoccupation with himself.

My brother, I'm not angry with you, we want to remain good friends, but don't pursue me with requests and mediation proposals that I will only have to reject. I will stay where I am. I beg of you to respect my freedom.

You stay where you are, it's best for you. Perhaps the news this letter brings will depress you even more. But I know you'll find comfort soon. Stay in the company most appropriate for your current disposition. I still love the fresh, natural sympathy, the free honesty that I know from August.

The comfort of your company and its apparent warmth do not beguile me. It is among us poor people, who are not chained by ceremony or prejudice, that I have discovered the freedom and naturalness of the real human being.

Farewell,

Clare

Postscript. I'm seeing more and more that I'm right, and that we can only keep ourselves from getting drunk if we hold on to ourselves and feel the human being in us. Little Clare has overcome the intoxication of employment and comfort. Humanity lives in her. I would never have believed that a woman could be such a true, honest person. This is my last philosophical lecture.

August

9. *The Final Scene*

(An audience with Herr Councillor, Gustav's father. In the beginning, only the following are present: the Councillor, the Councillor's Wife, and Karl.)

The Councillor: What do you think of this newspaper article? Mustn't every good Prussian heart feel offended when it sees how these super-clever ones, who will never understand anything about administration, take it upon themselves to hamper and complicate our activities with arrogant judgments?

Karl: You are right Herr Councillor. This article offers the most erroneous policy. It clearly promotes impractical fantasies of popular sovereignty, freedom, and equality, no matter how well the author has veiled them. All our corrections and amendments make little difference. These people refuse to be told what to do!

The Councillor: Sadly! Seeing articles like this appear almost daily, one almost wishes that this bad press would be thrown to the ground in one fell swoop and all at once, instead of still allowing it a minimal existence and irritating it with the pinpricks of censorship. But I don't want to appear dissatisfied with the administration either. They will use their wisdom to find the appropriate rules in good time.

Karl: And yet, I also believe that these articles are not really all that dangerous. They amount to empty shouting, which may sound unpleasant, but in the end has no effect whatsoever.

The Councillor: Probably true. But it's actually not the dangerous nature of these articles that upsets us, even if we would just prefer that such matters not come to light at all. Rather, it offends us that one dares to have an opinion next to the well-considered opinion of the government, and that, with this opinion, which is foolishly called "public opinion," one even claims to possess a kind of power. That annoys us. What is the point of these people when the administration is getting things done? You should only know what the government must take care of and monitor.

Karl: I won't say that one should allow the people their little pleasure, which they have when they hear themselves talk. But I want to express the hope that through uninterrupted activity, we will succeed in diminishing respect for these people in the eyes of humanity.

The Councillor: So, you admit that they still enjoy some kind of respect among the public? I don't even want to make that concession. The public has no opinion. Oh god. We find the press really troubling. After all, it is there, and so we would like to acknowledge it. Just not the way it is. I don't understand why this thing called the press does not, like everything else, bow to the demands and orders of the government. If things are going to be written and printed, why shouldn't the government employ people to supply that need in a genuinely loyal manner? If the government hires and trains teachers and professors and gendarmes, why shouldn't it hire writers too? If everyone who wants to give lessons must have a license, why not those who want to write? For writing is also a kind of teaching.

Karl: Well, that's where the censorship and the confiscation of books really helps.

The Councillor: But unfortunately, not enough! Writers nowadays grow up out of the ground like mushrooms. They make a formal trade out of writing, and yet they don't even need a trade license. Yes, it must come to pass that every writer is required to have a trade license. That would be a much better way of monitoring them than through censorship. Because, don't you see, things like this article still slip through. The press repeatedly fails to comply. It makes me anxious, because I absolutely do not understand it. We mean the people well. We want so badly to give them the genuine and loyal truth. Thus, we want to guide the press, and keep it on the right track. But just when we think we've gripped it tightly, it slips between our fingers. And all of a sudden what once seemed pious has changed into a venom-spewing serpent. The gentle Kreuzberg has transformed into a fire-breathing Vesuvius.[4]

Karl: I too believe there is still too much freedom of the press.

The Councillor: For example, the freedom from censorship for books over twenty sheets![5] If all books are to be supervised, why not these? If censorship is a sensible thing, why not censor all books? Why humor the dream of press freedom here while it is duly rejected there?

Karl: Hey, let's not be dissatisfied! Don't be dissatisfied! If in the end we can no longer cope, we must believe that everything will take care of itself.

The Councillor: That's my hope too. Perhaps in time all these people will give up their views, just as you were so fortunately cured of yours. Now, don't blush. You have no reason to be ashamed. To err is human.

The Councillor's Wife: But do tell me, Herr Karl. What did you actually believe when you thought you were a writer of the people? I must admit that I don't understand this expression! Who are your people? You see, as nobles, we pay very little attention to these modern views. We live so comfortably, nothing bothers us, and we can shrug them off. At most they are a minor annoyance. We are too content with our situation for such exaggerated fantasies to disturb our calm. And, believe me, our entire class thinks the same way. And now the middle class, the burghers, the artisans, they are far too busy with their businesses, or with building houses, or with raising families, to have time to read or think. And I doubt they would have understood you at any rate. So, who do you have left? The rabble? The poor mob? The proletarians? Now, thank God, they are too engrossed in worrying about their daily bread to be able to think of anything. The mob can't think! It belongs where it is! And so, who were your people? A chimera, a nothing! At most it was you and a few of your fellow true believers. And such a small handful of people wanted to cause such a large scandal!

Karl: Yes, I admit it, our thoughts were foolish fantasies, empty illusions in which we imagined ourselves who knows how big. We did not believe other than that, by bringing such universal ideas as state and freedom and justice and equality — ideas that live in the heart of every human being — into a people's consciousness, we could call a people to life.

The Councillor: Universal thought! Popular consciousness! Utter nonsense! I want to tell you something: There is no people, there are only estates. Look around you. Every class, every man has his own occupation, his own concerns, his own views. Everyone is concerned for his own welfare, and I can say that almost everyone feels satisfied with the lot that the Lord has assigned to him. He has his interests, he is permitted to have them, he must have them, and the police will help him protect them. How paternally our government cares for us! It spreads its protective wing over everyone, so long as he stays within his own circle. But in his circle, in his estate, he must remain. He should think himself neither too high nor too low. And that is what's right, that's the only way to have order, that's the only way to achieve peace. Quiescence is our first civic duty. Now notice how wrong you were. Everyone has and should have their own particular concerns, their particular interests. But how can one speak of universal ideas, of a people's consciousness? That's nonsensical. That instills far too much pride in the people, as if they were miraculous. And that is why those sayings are revolutionary and must not be tolerated.

The Councillor's Wife: Tell me, Herr Karl. Then, according to your earlier opinion, my cook would also have belonged to the people?

Karl: Certainly!

The Councillor's Wife: And me as well?

Karl: To my shame I admit it.

The Councillor's Wife: And we, my cook and I, would then have one and the same people's consciousness, as you called it?

Karl: Unfortunately.

The Councillor's Wife: One and the same. One and the same! Oh, that's terrible, that's outrageous. Yes, if you had shown us noble people consideration, if you had given us a different people's consciousness than our cooks. Then there would still be reason in it. But one and the same. What an outrageous thought!

The Councillor: And you don't know the worst of it. Herr Karl and those like him even dreamed of "the emancipation of women," as they put it. They did not want marriage. Instead, they wanted so-called free association. What didn't they want?

The Councillor's Wife: Well, if you haven't relinquished that thought, today you will receive a lesson that will command you forever. You will see a married couple that has no equal. Herr Baron Arthur and Marie, my niece, are coming here today. Now that is a pair! A unified harmony of souls! They live in undisturbed happiness! Everyone who knows her says: This is a beautiful couple, a true model couple.

The Councillor: And I thought you'd get married soon too, Herr Karl. He who does not take a wife and provide the state with excellent soldiers and clerks cannot be called a subject.

The Councillor's Wife: I also know a woman who is right for you. My maid is so good, so educated, though not beautiful. But even when she is married, she will be in my favor. Indeed, she will almost be a friend to me.

Karl: Oh, Sir and Madam, I am very touched by the kindness you are showing me. How shall I ever thank you?

The Councillor: Marry, and always remain true to your principles, live a life of solid principles.

(The Captain enters and greets the others.)

The Captain: I hear that Herr Gustav will be returning today from a short trip to the Berlin area — a little family reunion.

The Councillor's Wife: Yes, I don't know what drove him away, dear Gustav. He's been very mysterious lately. But I can count on him, he will quietly do good work. Oh, how virtuous my Gustav is!

(Gustav arrives. The Captain says to himself: "Speak of the devil." All greet each other loudly with expressions of joy. Gradually the Court Councillor, the Major, and the Cavalry Captain arrive. A general conversation ensues. Gustav, the Captain, and Karl step to a window.)

Gustav: I've wanted to ask you for some time, Herr Karl: what has happened to your sister? Has she rejected her past misery?

Karl: Do not talk to me about that wicked one.

(He inserts himself into a conversation with the others.)

The Captain: (Holding Gustav back, who wants to follow Karl.) Stay, Herr Gustav, I know everything. I take an interest in such things. I have made further inquiries and can give you all the information you can ask for. Karl had hardly moved into his new apartment when little Clare left him a few days later. No one knew why. I imagined a few things but was not about to speculate where I wasn't certain. But I also found out that she left the house immediately after meeting Baron Arthur on the stairs, who was going to visit the Councillor. I don't want to say that this encounter has any relation to her leaving. That's just a coincidence, a police indicium.[6]

Gustav: But where is the poor girl now?

The Captain: The poor woman returned to the shoemaker, where she used to live. The two appear very intimate. Of course, they have not been married, probably because the shoemaker can't afford the costs, or because little Clare considers it superfluous. She, as they say, manages his business.

Gustav: Oh, that ungrateful traitor. That twisted shoemaker. I should wring his neck!

The Captain: When she could have it so good . . . couldn't she, Herr Gustav.

Gustav: Oh, the shamelessness! I shall think of her no more, she is erased from my memory.

The Captain: Admittedly, she does not seem to have chosen a happy lot. Yesterday I saw her selling apples on the street corner. She must help the shoemaker!

Gustav: She is her own concern now, may she torment herself, she wanted it that way, and I wash my hands in innocence.

The Captain: Rightly so, Herr Gustav.

(Arthur and Marie enter. Arthur tenderly leads Marie by the hand, who gazes at him gratefully and kindly.)

The Major (to the Cavalry Captain): A beautiful happy couple! The Baroness knows how to behave so pleasantly, she also seems to be so devoted to her husband, that I gladly forgive her one mistake, her only misfortune — not being noble.

Arthur: Oh, I am your servant, Herr Karl. You've become solid — let's not discuss our earlier relationships or bygone stories. All is forgiven and forgotten. But I cannot refrain from expressing my joy that you have turned your back on your revolutionary ideas, indeed I hope that you will soon accept God. Just look at me and see what blessings come from a firm faith in God, a humble piety. I am content in myself. I have an honest wife who loves me. And I know how to keep myself from the sins of passion and haste. So, Herr Karl, my brother in Christ, I can't wish you anything better than to get married, return to God, and then to live as I do — a life of solid principles. But, Marie, my dear wife, you're not talking. We wouldn't want Herr Karl to think you are angry with him. Extend your hand in reconciliation and let this man know that you are happy.

Marie: Oh, you conceited one. Am I to trumpet your praise everywhere? Yes, Herr Karl, I am happy.

Karl: (To himself) The hypocrite. (Out loud) And I rejoice for your sake!

(The Privy Councillor arrives in a joyful mood.)

The Privy Councillor: Congratulate me, my brother-in-law, congratulate me, dear children, I've finally received a third-class medal.

(General excitement, congratulations, commotion. A group of relatives, including Karl, form around the Privy Councillor.)

The Privy Councillor: We should all be happy and see a life full of contentment ahead of us, because I am certain that sooner or later, I will also receive the Order of the Second Class. My luck greatly moves me, I can hardly find words and yet I want to keep talking. You, my children, bring me so much joy. Arthur, Marie, you love each other and thank me for marrying you. The government recognizes me. I am also completely reconciled with you, Herr Karl. Yes, yes, you also see now how the only concern of our government is to promote the happiness of its subjects. But she also stands firmly in the love and in the trust of her subjects. She knows how to punish wisely, and how to reward wisely. We are faithful to her, we love her, we serve her gladly, and pride ourselves in the obedience we render her. We call out with delight:

Long live solid principles!

Afterword

The Philosopher of Extremes
Edgar Bauer and the Birth of Anarchy

Charles Barbour

A Reckless Revolutionary

In November 1842, when the Young Hegelian movement was at the height
of both its influence and its notoriety, a long satirical poem titled *Die frech
bedräute, jedoch wunderbar befreite Bibel, oder, Der Triumph des Glaubens*
made something of a splash on the German and Swiss book markets. The topic
was the renegade theologian Bruno Bauer's recent and controversial dismissal
from the University of Bonn on the grounds that he espoused atheism, and the
polemics that ensued between his opponents and his defenders. While the poem
was published anonymously, it soon became known that it had been coauthored
by Bruno Bauer's younger brother Edgar Bauer and an emerging young journalist named Friedrich Engels. It consisted of four cantos written in tightly
measured heroic couplets. And it told the story of Bruno Bauer being tempted
away from God's side by the Devil, and of a great imaginary battle between the
conservative forces of Heaven, on the one side, and the revolutionary forces of
Hell, on the other. In God's army, Bauer and Engels located a host of powerful
(if now largely forgotten) theologians and historians including the Berlin professor and Bible scholar Ernst Hengstenberg, the Bonn professor and Christian
apologist Karl Heinrich Sack, and the historian and legal philosopher Heinrich
Leo. The Devil's army, on the other hand, consisted largely of Young Hegelian
writers and intellectuals, including Karl Marx, Ludwig Feuerbach, Max Stirner,
Ludwig Buhl, Eduard Meyen, Karl Köppen, Arnold Ruge, and, naturally, Edgar
Bauer and Friedrich Engels themselves. While elements of *Der Triumph des
Glaubens* are extremely clever, and might remind English-speaking readers
of mock epics like John Dryden's "Mac Flecknoe" or Alexander Pope's "The
Rape of the Lock," its wit relies on an enormous amount of context, and few
would confuse it with a great work of art. But it remains valuable today for its
humorous and informative portraits of the Young Hegelians — notably, in this
instance, its portrait of Edgar Bauer.

In the poem's third canto, then, as the forces of Heaven and Hell prepare to clash, Engels and Bauer take their place in the Devil's army alongside one another. And the two are immediately characterized (or rather, immediately characterize themselves) as the most diabolical of all the Young Hegelians, and the most willing to affirm revolutionary violence and Jacobin terror. Engels thus arrives on the scene plucking the strings of a guillotine like a harp and singing the revolutionary anthem "La Marseillaise" ("The song of hell always sounds, loudly he shouts the refrain / *Formez vos batallions! aux armes, citoyens!*"). Bauer's arrival is even more provocative, and it is worth quoting at length, as it offers unique insight into both his personal disposition and his political convictions:

> Who comes racing next to him, muscled like a brewer?
> Why that's bloodlust himself, that is Edgar Bauer.
> A stubbled beard does his brown face enfold,
> In years he is young, in cunning he is old.
> On the outside tails of blue, on the inside black and
>   chaotic,
> On the outside a man of fashion, on the inside
>   sans-culottic.[1]

The passage is, of course, saturated in irony. And throughout *Der Triumph des Glaubens* Bauer and Engels poke fun at their own revolutionary pretentions (and those of the Young Hegelians more generally) as much as they criticize the established order that was attempting to silence Bruno Bauer. But, in the mid-nineteenth century, to associate oneself — even jokingly — with the "bloodlust" of the "sans-culottes" was a profoundly dangerous, indeed reckless exercise. And, in a sense, recklessness was the dominant feature of Edgar Bauer's thought. It might even be characterized as his proposed strategy. For Bauer was, more than anything else, a philosopher of extremes. "Truth," he often declared, can only be found in "the extreme." For "only the extreme can take up a principle purely and carry it through; only the extreme and its principle have generative power."[2] Moreover, Bauer said, discovering the extreme and its principle was the purpose of "theory," which Bauer consistently privileged over what he saw as the impotent calculations, negotiations, and compromises of mere "practice" or the merely "practical." Indeed, on Bauer's account, "the true practice is theory," by which he meant doggedly pursuing the most radical position imaginable and articulating it openly and publicly with little or no concern for the consequences.[3]

Precisely because of this commitment to extremes, it is difficult to provide a concise overview of Bauer's career, or to capture his thought in a handful of statements. In his political theory in particular, his procedure consisted of submitting all established positions (from the most conservative to the most progressive) to what he called "ruthless" criticism.[4] And this frequently included the position that he himself had taken in his immediately previous work. Bauer's intellectual development can thus felicitously be characterized as one continuous effort at self-transcendence. He was, we might say, shamelessly avant-garde. He understood history as a process of relentless turbulence, motion, and change, and he self-consciously endeavored to be carried along by its force. We can already see this tendency on display in his earliest publication — an anonymous review of his brother Bruno Bauer's critical studies of the synoptic Gospels that appeared in Arnold Ruge's *Deutsche Jahrbücher* on November 1, 1841, under the title "Vorläufiges über Bruno Bauer, Kritik der evangelischen Geschichte der Synoptiker." Here the young Bauer developed an analogy between the, in his estimation, "revolutionary" theological and biblical criticism of David Strauss, Ludwig Feuerbach, and Bruno Bauer, on the one hand, and the events of the French Revolution, on the other. And he suggested that, while Strauss and Feuerbach were akin to the Girondins, or too willing to compromise and destined to get swallowed up by the forward march of events, Bruno Bauer was the contemporary Robespierre, or the one willing to follow the logic of history to its fearsome but inevitable conclusion. "In revolutions," Bauer declared, "victory and supremacy are only guaranteed to those who go furthest and develop the negative principle most sharply and consistently." "Moderates," he said a little later, "are always the victims of revolutions." And "truth can only win through struggle."[5]

Against the backdrop of this desire to "develop the negative principle most sharply and consistently," Bauer's writings during the 1840s — by far his most creative and productive years — can be roughly broken down into four components, each characterized, not only by a set of positive philosophical convictions, but also by a particular enemy or target. Initially, in 1842 and early 1843, Bauer pursued two overlapping lines of investigation. The first followed his brother closely, defended him in his struggles with the Prussian authorities, and mounted an attack on what he called "the Christian state." The position Bauer took in this work was explicitly revolutionary and republican, and its principal aim was to subordinate religious mysticism and particularism to a rational, universal, modern state. Over the same period, Bauer also developed an increasingly unique approach, challenging not only the conservative Christian state that was persecuting his brother, but also the, in his estimation, ineffectual gradualism and reformism of Germany's constitutional movements. Initially presented as a healthy debate among allies, Bauer's attack on constitutionalism reached a breaking point in his 1843 *Die liberalen Bestrebungen*, which argued that all right is derived from "the people," and that a free state could never be granted by existing powers, but only seized through confrontation and struggle. When the complete suppression of the Young Hegelian radicals in 1843 did not result in popular unrest, Bauer rapidly abandoned the figure of "the people," and political struggle more generally, and began to associate himself with proletarian social revolution, on the one hand, and a kind of proto-anarchism, on the other. This was the position set out in *Der Streit der Kritik mit Kirche und Staat*, the work that led to Bauer's arrest, trial, and imprisonment. Finally, through the course of his encounter with Prussia's legal and penal systems, Bauer's approach changed once again, as he became increasingly pessimistic about the prospect for collective struggle under modern conditions and adopted a more libertarian anarchist stance in which he privileged his own intellectual emancipation and the self-edifying pursuit of pure scientific truth.

What follows is divided into five sections. Each of the first four will be devoted to one of the components of Bauer's career outlined above. The fifth will briefly survey Bauer's work during and following the 1848 Revolutions, when he first lived in London as an exile and a spy for the Danish government, and then, after Prussian King Wilhelm I's 1861 amnesty for the 1848 revolutionaries, in Northern Germany, where he became founding editor of the conservative *Kirchliche Blatter*.[6] My approach will be intellectual historical. I will focus primarily on Bauer's published writings, with an eye toward locating his arguments within their immediate contexts. That is, borrowing a page from Quentin Skinner's work on method, I will interpret Bauer's texts, less as contributions to some centuries-old normative conversation concerning the ideal organization of human society, and more as performative speech acts intended to accomplish specific tasks within specific and specifically effective struggles and debates.[7] This seems to me to be a particularly appropriate way of studying Edgar Bauer and the Young Hegelians, as that was exactly how they understood their writings as well — not as placid descriptions of an existing state of affairs, but as polemical weapons designed to intervene in a battle. My aim, however, is not to be comprehensive. It is merely to offer an initial guide to Bauer's rich and compelling body of work, and to provide a foundation for further study. At the same time, while I will focus on historical reconstruction, my agenda is not exclusively historical. For whether we want to think of it as exemplary or cautionary, the story of Bauer's career provides crucial insight into the still very much alive question of the relationship between radical political theory, on one side, and concrete political institutions, on the other. Indeed, and as I shall suggest in my conclusion, the Young Hegelians' initial enthusiasm for, and eventual disillusion with, the modern state constitutes a crucial inflection point in the history of political thought, the consequences of which reverberated throughout the twentieth century and remain integral to our contemporary experience.

Partisan of the True State

Given that Edgar Bauer's earliest work is so heavily bound up with the defense of his brother, it is important to begin with a consideration of Bruno Bauer's thought, and how he came into conflict with the Prussian state. Bruno Bauer began his career as a Hegelian theologian and Bible scholar with a particular interest in religious history and the relationship between classical paganism, Jewish monotheism, and the Christian revelation.[8] Some of his earliest writings included critical reviews of David Strauss's *Das Leben Jesu*, in which Strauss argued that the Gospels were not eyewitness accounts of the life of Jesus but the collective myths of early Christian communities. Because of Bruno Bauer's challenges to his work, Strauss initially associated him with the so-called right Hegelians.[9] In fact, Bruno Bauer used his reviews of Strauss to introduce a theory of "self-consciousness" that would soon become integral to a larger, more radical political theological agenda.[10] The key texts signaling the emergence of Bruno Bauer's radicalism were his 1839 *Herr Dr. Hengstenberg* and his 1840 *Die evangelische Landeskirche Preußens und die Wissenschaft*. The former was a polemic that systematically dismantled the Christian apologetics and literalist Bible criticism of the powerful theologian named in its title. The latter developed an elaborate defense of King Friedrich Wilhelm III's efforts to unify Prussia's Lutheran and Calvinist congregations under a single state church. Because they were designed to intervene in complex and historically discrete debates, the implications of these works can be a little opaque from our current perspective. However, as Douglas Moggach has shown at some length, Bruno Bauer used them to promulgate a republican and revolutionary theory of state that his contemporaries recognized as a direct assault on the established order.[11]

The best way into Bruno Bauer's theory of state and the often dense political–theological arguments he employed to advance it is through a consideration of *Die evangelishe Landeskirche*. The same work offers insight into how Bruno Bauer pursued his revolutionary agenda, not in opposition to, but *through* the institutions of the Prussian state. Prussia's unified state church policy had been announced by Friedrich Wilhelm III in a Cabinet Order in 1817. Part of a larger program of administrative centralization, it curtailed the autonomy of the churches and gave the state the power to appoint ecclesiastical officials and dictate a uniform liturgy. For the same reason, it was vehemently opposed by religious nonconformists — so much so that, in 1834, the king was compelled to issue another Cabinet Order sanctioning the arrest of recalcitrant priests. Friedrich Wilhelm IV began his reign in 1840 with an effort to quell the tensions, including an amnesty for imprisoned clergy.[12] Defenders of the state church argued that it was primarily an administrative exercise aimed at rationalizing the relationship between the state and the churches. Bruno Bauer, however, proposed that the conservative critics of the union had in fact "seen more clearly," and that it was more profound and historically consequential than even its designers had understood. For, Bruno Bauer argued, with the union the spiritual power of religion was absorbed or "elevated" into the state, and the state became "the real presence of the rational and the divine." The union thus represented "the fact and the law of the Enlightenment in the church" and "the revolution perfected in the church."[13] Here, the obscure, otherworldly god of religion was replaced with "the idea of the God-humanity [*Gott-Menschheit*]."[14] Religious mysticism was finally and thoroughly subordinated to a rational public authority. And humans would no longer receive a revealed law from a heteronomous external source. Nor would they be divided by religious denominations. Instead, as active citizens of a free and universal state, they would autonomously and self-consciously create the laws that governed them.

The fact that Bruno Bauer developed his position by intervening in theological and ecclesiastical debates was not incidental. For one thing, and as Christopher Clark and others have argued convincingly, in Prussia during the early part of the nineteenth century, political questions were entirely inseparable from theological ones, and the power of the state was inextricably bound up with the power of the churches.[15] But more importantly, on Bruno Bauer's account, the enlighteners and revolutionaries of the eighteenth century — culminating in the Jacobins — had made the error of treating religion as an illusion, a fantasy, or even a deception intentionally invented by a priestly class to manipulate the people. In fact, and in Hegelian terms, religion was an element of a much larger historical process the purpose of which was the actualization of freedom and self-consciousness. It was thus not enough to expose religion as false. Instead, it was necessary methodically to work through its various manifestations and to show, with careful analysis, how it collapsed under the weight of its own internal contradictions. This was the project that Bruno Bauer took up most extensively in his critiques of the Gospels, and especially the three volumes of his *Kritik der evangelischen Geschichte der Synoptiker*, which appeared in 1841 and 1842, and which led to his confrontation with state authorities. For in those works Bauer argued, not only that the Gospels did not refer to any historical reality, but also that they were not myths of an early Christian community but the artistic creations of self-conscious individuals. And the only truth they contained was to be found in the very self-consciousness that had created them. The Gospels, in other words, were not descriptions of a divine being, but alienated expressions of the human capacity for free creation. And once that truth had been revealed, the whole history of religious experience that had taken shape around the Gospels could be absorbed back into its real human source.[16]

From the time of *Herr Dr. Hengstenberg*, Bruno Bauer's position within the Prussian university system was precarious. When the book appeared, Hengstenberg was the editor of the influential *Evangelische Kirchen-Zeitung* and a professor of theology at the University of Berlin, where Bruno Bauer was a private lecturer. To protect the young scholar from retaliation, the Prussian minister of culture and longtime patron of Hegelianism Karl Altenstein had him moved to the University of Bonn, where, after a probationary period, he was to be offered a chair in theology. But in 1840 both Altenstein and Friedrich Wilhelm III died. And Friedrich Wilhelm IV and his new Minister of Culture Friedrich Eichorn were much more suspicious of Hegelianism, especially the Young Hegelians. The publication of the first volume of Bruno Bauer's *Kritik der evangelischen Geschichte der Synoptiker* presented Eichorn with an opportunity to launch an investigation. Thus, on August 20, 1841, he solicited reports from a selection of Prussia's theology departments, asking them to respond to two questions: What was the theological position of Bauer's book? And could

Bauer continue in his position at the University of Bonn? The advice of the theology departments was mixed, and generally sought to balance the Protestant tradition of free scientific inquiry, on the one hand, with the principle that only those possessing a genuine faith could credibly teach young students of theology, on the other. Nevertheless, on March 29, 1842, Bruno Bauer was issued a letter indicating that his *licentia docendi* or license to teach in Prussian universities had been rescinded.[17]

Not long after, Bruno Bauer presented his assessment of this sequence of events, and what it meant for the Prussian state, in his *Die gute Sache der Frieheit*. In effect, he claimed that his dismissal from the University of Bonn represented the usurpation of state power by religion. In other words, and contrary to what had been called for in *Die evangelishe Landeskirche*, rather than the universal modern state subordinating and absorbing religion, religion had turned the state into an instrument that it could use to serve its particular ends. "In general," Bruno Bauer declared, "this is the collision: that the ecclesiastical and religious interests want to exert themselves at the expense of the concept of the state." In response, "the state must finally free itself from ecclesiastical and religious paternalism and constitute itself as a state." As Bruno Bauer saw it, his own "criticism" — the very thing that the regime was attempting to silence — was "the precondition for the endeavor of the state." For it alone "explains the ecclesiastical and religious power and completely dissolves its pretense to being an unearthly, superhuman power." And it alone "brings about the crisis that locates the purely human aspect of ecclesiastical and religious power in its proper place among the other human powers." The only remaining "question," Bruno Bauer concluded, "is whether the state should judge according to its real, free principle, or whether it is patronized by the church."[18]

Throughout 1842, Edgar Bauer wrote a series of articles on his brother's case for the *Deutsche Jahrbücher*, often using the anagram pseudonym "Dr. Radge." These articles consisted of critical reviews of works by other authors who had written on the issue. Toward the end of 1842, Bauer assembled and expanded on them in the volume *Bruno Bauer und Seine Gegner*, which was his first major work, and which appeared under his own name.[19] Many of the arguments Bauer developed there were closely related to those introduced in Bruno Bauer's *Die gute Sache der Frieheit*, including the notion that Bruno Bauer's dismissal proved that the Prussian state had relinquished its autonomy and become a mere instrument of religion — not a true or "free state," then, but a "Christian state." At the same time, the younger Bauer's rhetoric was much more incendiary, his political commitments much more explicit, and his central line of argument much more direct. Bauer began by asserting that "you cannot understand [Bruno] Bauer's affair unless you see that it concerns the nature of our time." "What is the nature of our time?" he continued: "It is revolutionary."[20] What followed was a protracted defense, not only of Bruno Bauer, but also of the concept of revolution. "Since childhood you have been frightened into immediately associating the idea of revolution with a bogeyman who comes with a guillotine and all kinds of atrocities in his wake," Bauer told his reader. "So, it is necessary to clarify this simplest and most innocent of all concepts and to rescue it from the hell to which it has been banished by the shortsighted and fearful."[21] The revolution, Bauer maintained, was nothing more than the replacement of old and imperfect forms with new ones. It was the inevitable engine of historical progress, and it followed directly from the logic of the Reformation. It was destructive, to be sure. But it destroyed only that which "wants to turn man, this spirit-filled creature, into a thoughtless and timid machine."[22]

Amid Bauer's detailed responses to his brother's opponents, two topics came to dominate *Bruno Bauer und Seine Gegner*: a republican conception of the state; and a valorization of principled extremism. In the first instance, Bauer maintained that the particular freedom of the individual and the universal freedom of the community were mutually reinforcing. For, in republican terms, genuine freedom could not mean independence from all interference. It could only mean relinquishing one's private, egoistic interests and participating in the public political life of the state. "In the true state," Bauer wrote, "each individual is consecrated by a civil consciousness [*bürgerliche Bewußtsein*], the consciousness of belonging to the universal human society that pursues rational human purposes. The fact that I am an organic part of a whole — which in its free liveliness stimulates, ennobles, and elevates the individual, stripping him of his selfishness — that I, acting for myself, at the same time act for a whole — is what gives me the character of a true citizen."[23] Here Bauer anticipated the reply — not uncommon at the time — that such a state would ultimately extend into every aspect of life, restrict subjective freedom, and become authoritarian.[24] And he effectively turned this argument back on the proponents of the Christian state:

> If we believed that the state had to take care of everything, we would not go beyond the Christian state. For the perfect Christian state is one where not a hair falls from the subject's head without the knowledge and will of the regent. Rather, we believe that the state, proudly conscious of its rationality, must find in freedom the element that teaches its citizens to be confident, bold, independent personalities. We believe that, by liberating every power of the individual, the state strengthens the power of the universal.[25]

The "true state," in other words, did not restrict the freedom of its citizens in any fashion. Rather, "it allows them to act freely and speak freely in the common consciousness that they are human beings."[26]

This brings us to the second topic mentioned above, or Bauer's valorization of principled extremism. In general, those who commented on Bruno Bauer's case fell into two camps: an orthodox group who thought it was patently absurd for an atheist to hold a position in a department of theology, and who applauded his dismissal; and another more conciliatory group, who defended his academic freedom but recommended he moderate his tone or present his findings in less stark terms.[27] *Bruno Bauer und Seine Gegner* certainly took aim at the first group. But it reserved special opprobrium for the second. For, on Bauer's account, what Bruno Bauer had discovered was not merely the truth about the origins of the Gospels, but a new historical principle — one that swept away religious consciousness and opened onto human freedom. And this development could not be mediated or moderated. On the contrary, Bauer maintained, "every new principle appears in world history as a vandal." It must "go to its most extreme development" and "unfold in its full truth" with "iron necessity."[28] "No external force can be imposed on it; no external law can inhibit it."[29] Thus, toward the end of *Bruno Bauer und Seine Gegner*, Bauer confessed: "What we are so often accused of is true — the new principle is sans-culottish. This means that the truth appears naked and uncovered, and the more ruthless it is, the more likely it is to win."[30] Despite the best intentions of his moderate defenders, there was no way of integrating Bruno Bauer's thought into the existing state of affairs. Indeed, for Bauer, "the mediators are the worst enemies of science."[31] Bruno Bauer's dismissal was not an oversight or an error that could be mitigated through careful argumentation. On the contrary, it was entirely consistent with the logic of the Christian state. Or rather, it exposed the inconsistency at the core of the Christian state. Here, Bauer concluded, "gentle reconciliation" was out of the question, and "only a battle of annihilation" could "bring the matter to an end."[32]

The revolutionary commitments expressed in *Bruno Bauer und seine Gegner* were amplified considerably in a bombastic book review that Bauer wrote for the *Deutsche Jahrbücher* at the very end of 1842. The book in question was a German translation of the Scottish historian Archibald Alison's *History of Europe from the Commencement of the French Revolution*. But the review was a pretext for Bauer to develop his own position. He began by ridiculing Alison's ideal of an "impartial historiography," particularly when dealing with an event like the French Revolution. "The revolution is still struggling, and the historian does not want to struggle," Bauer wrote. "She is in labor pains, and he wants to dissect her like a corpse." In fact, Bauer insisted, one could only understand the French Revolution by being a partisan, and by taking the side of either the "far left" or the "far right." For the truth of the revolution was only revealed in the extremes. Or, as Bauer put it: "Only the extremes know what they have in the revolution; for only they have a principle. Everything that lies between them is evil. Everything that lies between them is half-measured, fainthearted, and meek dawdling back and forth."[33] Bauer went on to attack Alison for transforming the great historical drama of the French Revolution into a paltry morality play, in which providence punished individual actors for their sins. "The moral view," Bauer maintained, "cannot rise to the perspective that sees man in the service of an idea." For "it wasn't people who were driven away by the revolution, but the opinions, the ideas of an entire bygone era. It wasn't people who were beheaded, but opinions and ideas of an old and a new time."[34] History, then, was not a scene of universal moral judgments, but a clash of incompatible theoretical principles. "The revolution cost a lot of blood, that is true," Bauer concluded, "but is there any theory that, if put into practice, would have celebrated a bloodless victory?"[35]

The Poverty of Liberalism

Bauer's rhetoric in works like *Bruno Bauer und Seine Gegner* and his articles for the *Deutsche Jahrbücher* — his refusal of "gentle reconciliation" and call for "a battle of annihilation" — placed him at odds, not only with the Christian state, but also, and perhaps more so, with much of its liberal opposition. More accurately, it thrust Bauer into a struggle that was taking place at the time over precisely what the term *liberal* was going to signify, and how it would come to operate in nineteenth-century political discourse.[36] Bauer was particularly concerned that this term — which in the early nineteenth century had much more radical connotations than it does today — would become conflated entirely with constitutionalism, and a model in which the state was understood, not as a political space in which citizens could exercise their public freedom or their capacity for collective self-determination, but as a means for securing the natural rights of the individual. We know from Bauer's correspondence that he was already preparing to challenge liberal constitutionalism in early 1842, when he informed his brother about a plan to write a polemic against Karl Rotteck's and Karl Welcker's *Staatslexikon* — an influential encyclopedia project that was used widely among German bureaucrats and businessmen, and that is often referred to as the "Bible" of Vormärz liberals.[37] The details of his challenge began to come into focus in a series of articles Bauer wrote for the *Rheinische Zeitung* in the summer of 1842, including "Die wahren Liberalen," "Fraktionen des Liberalismus," and "Das Juste-Milieu." It was then expanded and amplified in the two-volume study *Die liberalen Bestrebungen*, which appeared in early 1843 and took aim at liberal politicians in the Prussian province of East Prussia and the constitutional Grand Duchy of Baden.

The purpose of Bauer's pieces in the *Rheinische Zeitung* was to distinguish what he called "the true liberals" from all forms of moderation, especially constitutionalism. The argument was laid out most extensively in "Das Juste-Milieu," which consisted of two articles spread across five issues between June and August 1842. Significantly, when the second article appeared, the young Karl Marx, who was a contributor but not yet editor at the journal, wrote to the managing editor Dagobert Oppenheim to warn him against publishing such philosophically doctrinaire work. "Quite general theoretical arguments about the state political system are more suitable for purely scientific organs than for newspapers," Marx maintained. "The correct theory must be made clear and developed within the concrete conditions and on the basis of the existing state of things." Otherwise, the journal ran the risk of arousing "the resentment of many, indeed the majority, of the free-thinking practical people who have undertaken the laborious task of winning freedom step by step, within the constitutional framework, while we, from our comfortable armchair of abstractions, show them their contradictions."[38] But Bauer's point in "Das Juste-Milieu" was precisely that genuine freedom could not be won "step by step, within the constitutional framework," and that only an uncompromising theoretical stance was able to expose this ruse of practicality. Thus, Bauer argued that, under a constitution, "the state is divided into two camps," or the "chamber of deputies," which served the electorate, and "the government," which served the monarch. The two were meant to balance and check one another, but in fact they thwarted one another. There was thus "no principle of unity." What was worse, "all state institutions are regarded to exist only for the sake of security. They did not emerge from the spirit of the people; they are only there to limit two hostile powers that are forever at war."[39]

For Bauer, solving this dilemma required breaking definitively with all manifestations of social contract theory, and any notion that rights existed in a prepolitical state of nature. For the idea of a social contract rested on the assumption that the purpose of the state was either to limit or to secure those natural, prepolitical rights. But, on Bauer's account, "just as little as we can say that people have given themselves language through agreement can we claim that they entered society through a contract." Nature did not generate rights. Rather: "It is the education [*Bildung*] of society that first produces rights, and the greater this education is, the more the society approaches the state, and the greater, the more exalted are the rights of man. According to their essence, law and state are directly connected; no state without rights, no rights without a state, and therefore there are no natural rights."[40] Rights, then, were irreducibly social and political. They only existed in an organized political community. It followed that the basic and most primordial right was the right to belong to such a community or to be the citizen of a state and to participate directly in public life. Without this right, Bauer believed, freedom was an empty chimera.

As noted, Bauer developed and expanded this line of thought in *Die liberalen Bestrebungen*. Perhaps in response to the kind of criticisms Marx had raised in his letter to Oppenheim, he organized the work around analyses of two concrete political situations. The first volume, on "the East Prussian Opposition," thus focused specifically on the case of the liberal politician and cause célèbre Johann Jacoby, whose widely read 1841 book *Vier Fragen, beantwortet von einem Ostpreussen* had demanded that Friedrich Wilhelm IV fulfill his father's famous 1815 promise to grant Prussia a representative constitution and resulted in a protracted legal struggle between Jacoby and the Prussian regime (including a somewhat exaggerated charge of lèse-majesté, which potentially carried the penalty of death).[41] The second volume addressed "the Baden Opposition," and especially a complex series of events known as the *Urlaubstreit* or "vacation dispute," in which the Grand Duke of Baden's Minister Friedrich von

Blittersdorf sought to forestall the appointment of two liberal judges who had been elected to the parliament's Second Chamber by refusing to grant them "vacation" or leave from their positions in the state bureaucracy.[42] As Bauer saw it, both cases revealed the sheer futility of constitutionalism. In the first instance, Jacoby's project had been doomed from the outset. For genuine freedom could never be granted by a higher authority, given that the same authority would always retain the power to retract whatever right they had given. Similarly, the vacation dispute showed how, even in an established constitutional state, the arbitrary power of the sovereign and his ministers could bog opponents down in procedural issues and leverage the private interests of the people's representatives against the public good. For Bauer, then, constitutionalism had proven incapable of meeting the demands of the time. And any "true liberal" would have to discover a different path.

Apart from the detailed study of the East Prussian and Baden oppositions, *Die liberalen Bestrebungen* was primarily concerned with three issues: the revolutionary status of theory; the impossibility of legal reform; and the correct relationship between the people and the state. In the first case, Bauer noted that constitutionalism was presented by its defenders as the only "practical" approach. But, for Bauer, it was precisely this practicality that prevented it from accomplishing meaningful change. Being "practical," Bauer argued, was "delusional." It rendered you "dependent on the very system that punishes you" and "binds you to the enemy." Under current conditions, then, "the true practice is theory."[43] For "theory is proud and independent." It "makes us despise every contract and every mediation" and "teaches us the real decisive hatred" required for a "violent and irresistible break" with what exists.[44] The same principle applied to Bauer's rejection of any notion of legal reform. "Laws," Bauer argued, "are and can be nothing more than an expression of the conditions in which they are created." Thus, any dismantling of "the old conditions" also required a dismantling of "the old laws." And "a legal reform" was "a contradictio in adjecto." It was, as Bauer colorfully put it, "a guillotine without the falling blade [*Guillotine ohne Fallbeil*]."[45] The juxtaposition of the French and German words for guillotine in this passage was meant to imply that Germany's legal reformers were attempting to achieve the results of the French Revolution without the accompanying violence and terror. For Bauer, that project was futile. The only way forward was the complete negation of the established order, and the pursuit of what Bauer explicitly called a "revolutionary republican" alternative.

This brings us to the third claim mentioned above, or what Bauer took to be the correct relationship between the people and the state. Here Bauer returned to the theme that he had introduced in "Das Juste-Milieu" of the divided nature of constitutional orders. The case of the *Urlaubstreit* revealed how the constitutional separation of powers between elected representatives and appointed ministers and officials did not mediate political contradictions but submerged them in an absurdly complex proceduralism that rendered their resolution impossible. The way forward, Bauer believed, was to do away with any notion of the division of powers and to have the state reflect the unified will of the people. Here, rather than the people seeking representation *within* the state, the two — the people and the state — would become indistinguishable. As Bauer put it: "It is not enough for the people to take part in the state." Rather, "the people should be the whole state." To have a "truly popular government," Bauer said, "the people must be the only source of all power and all right." And in that case:

> There is no longer any talk of two enemy powers, no more subjugation of one power to another, because the government resulting from the unity [*Einen*] of the people will never be in opposition to the officials, who owe their origin to the same power. . . . Then the people's representation no longer has the false sense of a guarantee against the overarching arbitrariness of an independent governing power, but rather becomes the representative of state reason [*Staatsvernunft*], the embodiment of the people's intelligence.[46]

As Bauer knew, the standard argument against this conflation of the people and the state was that it had no robust conception of institutions, and no viable theory of political representation. It suggested a kind of direct democracy that was untenable in large modern states. For his part, Bauer did not hesitate to address this issue head-on. "Even a pure republic can have representation," he wrote. But in a republic, there was no difference between the people's representatives and the governmental ministers or officials. Indeed, Bauer declared, "in the republic there is no government [*Regierung*] at all, but only an executive power [*ausführende Gewalt*]." And this executive power had no "independent force [*Macht*] over the people, independent principles, or independent officials" but found "the source of its power and its principles in the supreme state power, in the people."[47]

Bauer reinforced this republican theory of the state in two shorter pamphlets he wrote in early 1843: *Georg Herwegh und die literarische Zeitung*, which addressed the expulsion of the writer Georg Herwegh from Prussia and the way it was reported on in the conservative *Literarische Zeitung*; and *Staat, Religion und Parthei*, which was a programmatic discussion of political parties and state forms. Herwegh was a wildly popular political poet who, while touring Prussia in late 1842, was called to a private audience with Friedrich Wilhelm IV. Soon after the meeting, he wrote a letter to the king aggressively criticizing his failure to institute freedom of the press. On December 24, 1842, a leaked copy of the letter appeared in the *Leipziger Allgemeine Zeitung*. As a result, the journal — which had been an important organ for the radical movement — was banned in Prussia, and Herwegh was threatened with arrest and forced to flee to Switzerland.[48] Bauer's intervention was a response to the *Literarische Zeitung*'s defense of the king's actions. Normally, Bauer began, he would not consider the journal "worthy of refutation." But in its attack on Herwegh it had outlined a concept of "freedom" that helpfully exposed the errors of its "worldview."[49] For the *Literarische Zeitung*, then, freedom or independence was an obvious good. But it also presupposed a society in which all individuals were dependent on someone. And this necessarily entailed a hierarchy, as some were more dependent, some less. Like the father in a family, the king was the one on whom all others were dependent. On this account, Bauer retorted, "the state is nothing but a private agreement, nothing but the accidental result of an accidental power." Here "law and justice are not the expressions of common reason, but rather services that power gives me at will in return for my services." Bauer continued:

> No one who pays homage to such a view will ever understand what true freedom entails. For he only knows the freedom of the private person, the independence that I enjoy in the particular; but he does not see that I also want freedom in the universal, freedom as a state-citizen [*Staatsbürger*]. And this freedom consists in the fact that I recognize my own will in the laws of the state and common reason in its institutions; that my true existence, my spiritual one, is not inhibited by paternalism or oppressed by raw power.[50]

Freedom, in other words, had nothing to do with either dependence or independence. It involved participating in the formulation of the laws that governed one's community. Under these conditions, "the people love the laws because they are the laws, and because they gave them to themselves." And the state was "not a private institution run by private people, but rather a rational whole, a rational universal community."[51]

Staat, Religion und Parthei, which was inscribed "Berlin, March 10, 1843," began with another appeal to the superiority of theory over practice. "Despite all our cleverness," Bauer declared, "we don't think our theory is nearly theoretical enough." It went on to break the contemporary political scene down into three groups: "the liberals"; "the legitimists"; and "the radicals."[52] To each of these groups, Bauer assigned a conception of the state and a corresponding attitude toward both religious confessions and political parties. Thus, "the liberals" were associated with "The State of Commonsense," in which the state was understood to be a neutral container of all confessions and opinions, provided those remained within the realm of private life. "The legitimists," on the other hand, pursued "The State of Individuality," in which the state was dominated by the personality of the king, excluding all other parties and confessions. Finally, "the radicals" were said to promote "The State of Principles." On this model, Bauer claimed, "the commonsense distinction between private and political conviction is abolished as is the unconditional surrender of man to the will of an individual." As a result:

> Private consciousness and political consciousness collapse into one. Everything I do, I do as a citizen, and the universality of the state takes up my entire being. The state is neither a rigid,

> abstract power that controls and governs me for my own good,
> nor an otherworldly being to which I bow in humility. Here I
> know of no such higher, foreign ideal at all, since the purpose,
> function and essence of the state lives and runs in my person-
> ality, and the ideal of the state has passed into my flesh and
> blood.[53]

The citizens, in other words, would relinquish their particular private interests
and orient themselves toward the universal, and the state would become nothing but the active participation of the citizens in public life. But what would be
the fate of political parties in such a state? What would be the fate of difference
and debate? "There will be parties as long as there are states," Bauer explained:

> But there is a big difference whether all parties are recognized
> and discussed, or whether only one is seen as legitimate and
> therefore completely identified with the state. If the former is
> the case — and it is the case in the principled state — then the
> government [*Regierung*] would not have to turn now here and
> then there, now to consult the opinion of this side and now that
> side. Rather, the government will emerge as an organic growth
> from the life of the state. And this life consists of nothing other
> than the mutual competition of the parties, which, as each party
> is allowed to express itself and develop all its strengths, will
> always reveal the true content, the true spirit of the state.[54]

For Bauer, then, the ideal republican state was a radical, agonistic democracy
energized by the civic virtue of its citizens, in which all matters of public consequence would be submitted to open debate and vigorous struggle between a
multitude of political parties — parties that represented, not private or particular interests, but different conceptions of the public good, or different under-
standings of how such a universal good might be achieved.

But this approach to the state, which had taken shape in Bauer's work over
the course of little more than a single year, would not last long. The suppression
of the Young Hegelian movement in early 1843 was swift and decisive. In late
1842, the *Deutsche Jahrbücher* was banned in Prussia, and in January 1843,
the regime of Friedrich Wilhelm IV was able to use its influence in Saxony to
stop it from being printed there as well. Despite protestations from the powerful businessmen who financed it, by March 1843, the *Rheinische Zeitung* had
also been forced to close its doors. Worse still, on January 31, 1843, the king
issued a Cabinet Order intended to clarify his attitude toward censorship and to
place strict limits on the range of acceptable public discourse. On February 4,
1843, that Order was backed up by a more detailed Censorship Instruction that
restructured the censorship authority and installed a new Ober Censurgericht
or Higher Censorship Court with the power to prosecute anyone who sought to
publish without the permission of the government and to impose long prison
sentences on offenders.[55] A division that had been taking shape within the

movement for some time between the more strategic faction organized around Ruge and Marx, on the one side, and the more outspoken Berlin faction known as "the Free," on the other, finally resulted in a split. Ruge and Marx moved to Paris, where they initially planned to continue the political struggle from exile with their *Deutsch–Französische Jahrbücher* (the journal lasted just one double issue before its editors also came into conflict), while the Bauer brothers and their followers decided to stay in Berlin and continue fighting the censorship head-on. At the same time, Bruno Bauer and Edgar Bauer initiated a process of self-criticism, especially around what they now thought of as their misguided faith in the rational nature of the state, or the possibility of achieving revolutionary ends through its mechanisms. As both brothers noted, the Young Hegelian project prior to 1843 had consisted of one long paean to the greatness and glory of the state, which they believed would ultimately have no choice but to listen to reason and science. In response, the state had been used to crush them — to close their journals, destroy their academic careers, ban their books, and in many cases either chase them into exile or cast them into dungeons. To be certain, their revolutionary commitments were going to live on. But the notion that the state would be the primary lever of the revolution disappeared for good.

Anarchy and the Free Society

In the opening months of 1843 Bauer momentarily set aside his work on political theory to compose the novella *Es leben feste Grundsätze!* Not insignificantly, the story concerned the disillusion of a young political radical living in Berlin during the early 1840s and working as a writer for journals including the *Rheinische Zeitung*. As I pointed out in the preface to this volume, Herbert De Vriese has recently made a strong case for the argument that Bauer's character "Herr Karl" was based on Karl Marx, and that the novella can be read as an act of literary revenge for Marx's public attacks on "the Free."[56] But the experience of a political loss of faith was not entirely something that Bauer had to project onto Marx. For precisely at this moment in his life, it was just as much (if not more) something he was experiencing as well. How to continue to pursue a revolutionary agenda now that the state and the political sphere in general had revealed themselves to be beholden to the forces of reaction became the question at the center of Bauer's next major work — *Der Streit der Kritik mit Kirche und Staat*. As the preeminent German scholar of Young Hegelianism Wolfgang Eßbach has noted, many of the theoretical innovations often attributed to Marx, and to his so-called "break" with the Young Hegelians (including the concept of a social revolution, the historical mission of the proletariat, and the critique of utopianism), were anticipated by Bauer in this volume, so much so that it seems at least plausible that Marx was developing his ideas through a sotto voce engagement with Bauer's work.[57] But questions of priority notwithstanding,

Der Streit der Kritik mit Kirche und Staat is a significant piece of political theory independent of any influence it might have had on Marx, and, like many of Bauer's writings from the 1840s, it deserves to occupy a more prominent position in the history of political thought.

If the target of *Bruno Bauer und Seine Gegner* was the Christian state, and that of *Die liberalen Bestrebungen* was the liberal constitutionalists, Bauer began *Der Streit der Kritik mit Kirche und Staat* by proposing that the "tyranny" of "cross" and "throne" relied on the apathy and indecisiveness of a new enemy, namely the people themselves, or those whom Bauer now referred to as "the mass." "With a tremendous force of inertia," Bauer wrote, "an uneducated and selfish mass can hold on to what exists simply because it exists." And Bauer wasted no time applying this criticism to his imagined reader:

> You yourselves have a police sentiment [*Polizeigesinnung*] so you are not treated like a free people. You do not allow your thoughts to be expressed within yourselves, and that is why the government is permitted to suppress the free expression of ideas. You yourselves are quite comfortably occupied with your individual and bourgeois affairs; you know nothing of the high and human questions of freedom. And that is why the government treats you as individuals, supervised and lovingly attached to a police guard.[58]

As Bauer saw it, the solution to this dilemma was an unflinching voluntarism. It was not, in other words, to request or even demand freedom, but immediately to take it, and in taking it, to enact or perform it. "The tyranny, the physical and moral pressure that you suffer, has its origin and meaning only in your weak mind," Bauer insisted. "Do not censor yourself and you will not be censored. Be free yourself and you will be able to fight for freedom. Cast off your petit-bourgeois attitude, become human beings, and you will gain recognition of your human rights."[59]

With that strategy in the background, a significant portion of *Der Streit der Kritik mit Kirche und Staat* rehearsed the details of Bruno Bauer's critique of religion and the debates surrounding his dismissal from the University of Bonn. Bauer justified returning to these issues by suggesting that the critique of religion remained a powerful foundation for any further investigations. As Bauer put it: "The critic who has destroyed the sanctity of faith has an even easier job if he also wants to prove invalid the sanctity of political institutions."[60] At the same time, the title of *Der Streit der Kritik mit Kirche und Staat* alone suggested a new approach was in store. Thus, Bauer declared that: "Above all, I have endeavored to be more precise in my criticism of the existing state conditions, because I am convinced that criticism in general will turn more and more from theological to political and social questions."[61] And, when compared to Bauer's previous work, precisely this was the innovation of the book. Rather than challenging the Christian state from the perspective of a true, free, or ideal republican state, or seeking to subordinate religious mysticism to a rational public authority, Bauer was now critical of the very concept of the state and convinced that freedom was incompatible with such an institution. The state, in other words, was no longer the actualization of reason in the world. It no longer represented the institutional and normative framework in which citizens could directly participate in formulating the laws that governed their community. Its instrumentalization by religion during the course of the Bruno Bauer affair had exposed it as an instrument of power. And any other conclusion was utopian.

Perhaps in an effort to conceal it from the censors, this new, proto-anarchist commitment was laid out most explicitly toward the very end of the volume, and particularly in three sections titled "The Political Revolution," "The Free Society," and "Peace" respectively. The first of these began by addressing the common accusation that Bauer and his associates wanted to revisit the French Revolution and that they were essentially modern Jacobins enamored with Robespierre and the events of 1793. In fact, Bauer replied, they were of the opinion that the Jacobins had failed, and even that their errors had led to the Napoleonic Empire and the Bourbon Restoration. But that failure had been the effect of their inability to go beyond the state and the merely political revolution. The Jacobins "believed that true freedom could be realized in the state." And therefore, they could not understand "that all efforts for freedom were essentially against the state."[62] Bauer continued: "If the political revolution does not know how to overcome itself, if it does not know how to move past the abstraction of the state and toward the understanding of full common freedom then it will always return to the legitimacy and tyranny of stability."[63] The best proof of this principle was the fate of France following the 1830 Revolution, where the state had become thoroughly controlled by a wealthy bourgeois class, and the people fixated entirely on their own narrow private interests. "That is where the constitution [*Constitution*] leads and that is where it must lead," Bauer claimed. "Given time, it will become just as oppressive as any other state formation [*Staatsverfassung*]."[64]

The same logic that led Bauer to reject political revolution and the concept of the state compelled him to abandon the other concept that had been so integral to his earlier work, and especially *Die liberalen Bestrebungen*, namely the concept of "the people." This project was central to the second section mentioned above, or "The Free Society." "People," Bauer argued, "is a political concept, a word of the heart." Far from being inherently revolutionary: "The people are the trusting crowd that allows themselves to be guided. What prevents a tyrant from carrying out his deeds in the name of the people? What prevents a people from standing up and shedding their blood for a ruling family? The concept of freedom is not included in the political concept of the people."[65] There was, moreover, nothing essential binding the people together, and no substance behind the accidental fact of their common geography and customs. "The people is but an external union, a convoluted group of estates and individuals, conceived of on this particular soil, in this climate, raised according to these laws.

Its outward representation is only found in a certain national pride and national quirks." As a result, "in a free community there is no longer an exclusive people."[66] But, if not a state and not a people, what would form the basis of a "free community" or "free society"? How would it be organized and according to which ideals? On this issue, Bauer was decidedly evasive. "It is not our job to construct," he wrote. For no one can "think beyond their time." And "our time is only critical and destructive."[67] The new free society would have to be discovered through free revolutionary process, and only its bare skeleton could be stated in advance: "No private property, no privilege, no distinction of status [*Standes*], no usurpative government. This is our pronunciamento. It is negative," Bauer acknowledged. "But history will write its affirmation."[68]

By far the most belligerent part of *Der Streit der Kritik mit Kirche und Staat* was the final section, ironically titled "Peace." It was here that Bauer took up the cause of the poor (or those whom he variously called the "rabble [*Pöbel*]" and the "propertyless [*Besißlosen*]") and predicted that they were historically destined to lead a social revolution — one that swept away "state society" and found a new community of freedom and equality. Bauer began by defining both terms in his own manner. Freedom, he claimed, was not a positive condition to be achieved, but an essentially destructive force. It "does not create conditions but only abolishes them." It "does not make people satisfied but only dissatisfied." It "shocks people out of their calm and drives them forward." "Freedom will therefore have an effect in history as long as there is history." "When we therefore speak of a free state that humanity should achieve, we mean nothing more than that humanity should no longer be separated and dominated by the state but should gain the ability for the uninhibited pursuit of historical truth in common and without aristocracy. We believe that humanity is only free when it has accepted everyone into an equal alliance and when it has made the historical struggle a struggle between equals."[69] Freedom, then, was inseparable from equality. And by this Bauer meant, not formal legal equality, but material as well as intellectual equality. "What does abstract equality before the law mean," Bauer asked, "when this law is unjust and when it ascribes the advantages of property [*Besißes*] and education [*Bildung*] to a few, but forces the vast majority to suffer, to work anxiously for a meager existence, and to abstain from thinking?"[70] Real equality therefore required the abolition of property as well as the presupposition that all individuals — without exception, including the poor — were capable of the cultural education and rational deliberation required to participate meaningfully in public life.

Bauer's attack in this passage on the principle of "abstract equality before the law" — his suggestion that, in a society based on the unequal distribution of property and education, legal equality amounted to an empty ruse — had an antinomian flavor, and it contributed to a critique of law that had been taking shape in his work since *Die liberalen Bestrebungen*. At the same time, it is important to note that these comments were themselves framed by a larger affirmation of juridical categories, and especially the concepts of justice and right.

In other words, in contrast with the approach that Marx and Engels would soon develop in the manuscripts now known as *The German Ideology*, Bauer did not yet go so far as to reduce law to a more fundamental social or material reality. Rather, he argued that law within the state had become a corruption of its genuine essence. For "the state makes right the prerogative of egoism" and combines "law" with "paternalism and oppression." But "the very concept of right and law presupposes universality." It was thus inevitable that, "in opposition" to law as it had developed in the state, "the consciousness of truly universal and communal rights must finally arise and lead the propertyless [*Besißlosen*] to revolt against the propertied [*Besißer*]."[71] Exactly what institutional or practical form "truly universal and communal rights" would take, Bauer did not say. But — in a manner that would seem difficult to square with his comments on contract theory and natural rights in "Die Juste-Milieu" — he now seemed to approve of the idea that something like right could exist independent of the state. Or at any rate, his prediction of an impending social revolution relied on a rhetoric or an idiom of rights, even if he could say very little more as to how they would be grounded or what they would entail.

In August 1843, Prussian police seized all copies of *Der Streit der Kritik mit Kirche und Staat* before they could be distributed. An investigation ensued, and on October 23, 1843, the Ober Censurgericht brought criminal charges against both Edgar Bauer and his brother Egbert, who had served as the publisher of the book. Edgar Bauer's trial took place over multiple sessions between October 1843 and May 1844, when he was finally convicted of insulting religious society, mocking the law, arousing dissatisfaction with the state, and offending the majesty of the king. He was then sentenced to eight years in prison — a punitively long time even by contemporary standards. Almost as soon as the verdict was announced, and in a move that caught the court by surprise, Bauer and his followers published the proceedings of his trial (including transcripts of the judges' numerous interrogations of him) in Switzerland in a volume called *Preßproceß Edgar Bauers, über das von ihm verfaßte Werk: Der Streit der Kritik mit Kirche und Staat*. Among other things, these documents revealed how Bauer was able to use the court as a platform to articulate and reinforce the very views that the court was seeking to suppress, and his responses to his inquisitors provide both a summary of his position and a record of his courage and defiance. Bauer's basic strategy was to deny the court and the law any jurisdiction over his work, which he described as purely scientific and literary in nature, concerned only with historical truth, and disinterested in any practical political consequences. "I do not compose my work with regard to the state laws but from science and its results," Bauer declared. "If criticism collides with the law, that is precisely the fault of the law":

> If I now prove that the state owes its origin to egoism, if I prove
> the limited nature of the state's existence, if I prove that the state
> structure and state law are only designed for that egoism, the

> main product of which is private property, if I further explain
> that egoism and its institutions will never be able to give them-
> selves up on their own, if I draw the conclusion from all this
> that respect for the law and private property, respect for what
> exists, will be destroyed, that anarchy must inevitably set in as
> the beginning of a new human life, these claims still remain
> within the scope of literary evidence, and I can recognize in
> them no other opposition than literary.[72]

When accused of inciting violence, Bauer argued that the state itself was essentially violent, and that "the proceedings against me prove these statements to
be correct." Indeed, Bauer maintained, "if I draw the undeniable conclusion
that violence and egoism can in turn only be defeated with violence" then this
conclusion could not justifiably be blamed on him, but only "on egoism itself"
or "on history for demanding bloodshed to progress."[73]

Bauer's defense, then, was an enactment of the voluntarism he recommended
to his reader in *Der Streit der Kritik mit Kirche und Staat*. When brought before
the court, he treated his freedom, not as a request or even a demand that he
could make on the state, but as an axiom or presupposition that he would exercise or perform. If the state claimed that he had disrespected its institutions,
then he insisted that the state first prove "that what I am said to have treated
disrespectfully is worthy of respect." If the state wanted to subject him to the
judgment of the law, then he insisted that the state first prove "that the laws and
conditions of the Prussian state should not be subjected to the judgment of the
critic."[74] The accusations made against Bauer showed that what he had said
about the state was true. Thus, he could only defend himself by repeating the
ostensible crimes for which he had been brought to trial. "I too want nothing
but freedom and real progress," Bauer maintained. The court replied that "freedom lies within the laws." "But I believe I have the right to define freedom and
progress in my own, that is scientific and critical way." And moreover, such a
"critical and open definition as mine requires an equally open refutation before
the public, not an investigation within the four walls of a courtroom."[75] This
attitude was carried forward to Bauer's final statement, which he signed on
May 5, 1844: "I have described religion, the Christian state, and the theological
government. Whether this offends religious societies, impudently mocks the
law, arouses displeasure, or insults majesties is irrelevant to criticism and to its
knowledge." Indeed, Bauer concluded: "All the crimes I have been accused of
can be reduced to one: I am a writer and know only the laws of literature. The
High Court must now decide whether it wants to condemn literature."[76]

The Science of Self-Liberation

We noted earlier that, when the Young Hegelian movement splintered in early
1843, the Berlin faction around the Bauer brothers did not follow other radicals

into exile but made a point of remaining in Germany to face the new censorship laws directly. Their main organ during this period was the *Allgemeine Literatur-Zeitung* — a monthly journal that began appearing under Bruno Bauer's editorship in December 1843. The first eight numbers of this journal supplied the target for Marx and Engels's well-known polemic against the "critical critics" in *The Holy Family*. But while Marx and Engels's scornful reading of the *Allgemeine Literatur-Zeitung* has been influential (and heavily determined the way that the Young Hegelians were perceived during the twentieth century), a closer examination of the original material shows that their approach was more than a little incomplete. The central agenda of the *Allgemeine Literatur-Zeitung* was articulated concisely in an advertisement for it that appeared at the time. It was, as the advertisement read, "to illustrate the inner weakness of the political enlightenment of 1842, and therefore to explain its downfall."[77] The project, then, was self-critical. Former partisans of "the political enlightenment of 1842" (or Young Hegelians) would admit that their failure had been caused, not simply by an arbitrary and overpowering external authority, but by their own "inner weakness." Bruno Bauer developed this idea more systematically in his "Was ist jetzt der Gegenstand der Kritik?," which was published in the journal in July 1844. Referring to the rapid destruction of Young Hegelianism in early 1843, Bruno Bauer wrote: "The mass of enlightened people could only collapse so decisively after the external blow because they had already collapsed into themselves beforehand."[78] "The political enlightenment of 1842," in other words, had been founded on a crucial error — namely the belief in the inherent rationality of the state and of political life in general. Because of this misplaced faith, it did not portend a revolutionary people capable of participating in the formation of the laws that governed them, but a docile mass willing to allow the state to regulate and administer every aspect of its existence.

Among Edgar Bauer's numerous contributions to the *Allgemeine Literatur-Zeitung*, three stand out: a serialized short story called "Die drei Biedermänner," which appeared across three issues in early 1844; a piece titled "Proudhon," which consisted of translations of large sections of Proudhon's 1841 *Qu'est-ce que la propriété?* interspersed with critical commentary; and, most importantly, a longer essay named "1842," in which Bauer reflected on the fate of what Bruno Bauer had dubbed "the political enlightenment" of that year. "Die drei Biedermänner" told the story of three well-meaning liberals — an "old man," a "thin man," and a "doctor"[79] — seeking to understand the growing mass of urban poor. Rather than studying the issue abstractly, they agreed that it was necessary to circulate amid the poor and encounter their real conditions. In short, each one of them was cleverly swindled by the ones they condescendingly set out to assist — Bauer's theme being the inadequacy of liberal charity in the face of a new destitute class and the superior intelligence of the members of that class. Significantly, Bauer's reflections on "Proudhon" were coeval with the emergence of the so-called True Socialist movement, and the argument that Moses Hess and Karl Grün would make for combining Feuerbach's theory and

Proudhon's practice.[80] A significant amount of Marx's contribution to *The Holy Family* also consisted of an elaborate, often malicious response to Bauer's analysis in this piece.[81] In essence, Bauer argued that Proudhon was insufficiently dialectical and historical — that he relied on a transcendental concept of "justice," which he considered "an absolute eternal basis for history,"[82] and that he treated property as merely false, or an inauthentic form of human existence, rather than a historically necessary aspect of human development. The proposal, then, was that Proudhon should school himself in philosophy. And, not incidentally, that is exactly what Proudhon did for his 1846 *Système des contradictions économiques ou Philosophie de la misère*, or the work that inspired Marx's polemical *Poverty of Philosophy*.

The essay "1842" — which was the lead article in the July 1844 number of the journal, or around the same time that Bauer was sentenced to prison — was in many ways a pivotal text in Bauer's career. For it was here that he first fully and publicly disavowed his earlier commitment to radicalism and rejected any emancipatory politics. "The year 1842," Bauer began, "was liberal." However, he continued, "the critical opposition to liberalism, which called itself radical, was nothing but further-reaching liberalism."[83] The liberals wanted to expand the scope of politics and sought more equitable political representation. The radicals, pushing the matter further, wanted to make politics thoroughly universal, or render the state absolute. The radicals thus argued for extending the logic of greater representation to that of universal participation. And their basic demand was for all of the people to be actively engaged in the political life of the state all of the time. But now the abject failure of this approach was undeniable. For not only had the state been used to destroy the radicals. It had done so with the approval — or at least docile acquiescence — of the people. As Bauer put it, in crushing the Young Hegelian movement or "the political enlightenment of 1842," "the government thus proved that its strength was undiminished and, above all, that it still enjoyed the same support among the people as it always did." Consequently, "criticism had to relinquish its opposition to the government, its demand for the free state, and, at the same time, its appeal to the people." In short, "it had to stop being political." Thus, Bauer declared: "Criticism has ceased to be political. Previously it fought views through views, systems through systems, attitudes through attitudes. Now it becomes without views, systems, or attitudes. Previously it appealed to the sacred interests of the people and recognized its highest power in the people. Now it recognizes the political unity of the people and the government."[84] To be certain, some could still be heard demanding that "criticism offer something new," and especially that it present "a brand-new socialist system for their beloved people." But those who made such demands "only reasserted the interests of the indolent masses."[85] The proper response to the current situation was not the formulation of yet another political dogma, Bauer concluded, but the repudiation of all politics and all dogmas.

Here it is important to point out that, while the Bauer brothers' approach at this moment certainly had an element of the apolitical quietism and Olympian disdain for the masses of which Marx and Engels accused them in *The Holy Family*, it was also designed to be provocative. As Hegelians, both Bruno Bauer and Edgar Bauer were consistently anti-utopian. For them, the actuality of the situation was historically determined and had to be interrogated and negotiated on its own terms. The reality was that the new censorship legislation and the regime of Friedrich Wilhelm IV had eliminated the possibility of transforming the Prussian state through political engagement, which had been the struggle in 1842. But if the critic now spoke only scientific truth, and if this still generated a censorious reaction from the state, then that would expose the state to be the enemy, not only of this or that political faction, but of the truth as such. To this end, Bruno Bauer and Edgar Bauer produced large, multivolume historical studies of the Enlightenment, the French Revolution, and modern German history, including a history of the party struggles of 1842. All of these were primarily factual. But because of the authors and the topics, all were also implicitly threatening to the established order.[86] While Bruno Bauer was the primary force behind these studies, Edgar Bauer contributed, sometimes as coauthor, sometimes as the sole author. The ones he wrote on his own included the first volume of the study of the French Revolution, titled *Die constituirende Versammlung vom October 1789 bis zur Flucht Ludwigs XVI* and the third volume of the history of modern Germany, or *Geschichte der constitutionellen und revolutionären Bewegungen im südlichen Deutschland in den Jahren 1831–1834*. The scholarly rigor of these endeavors should not go unnoticed. Indeed, the study of the constitutional and revolutionary movement in Southern Germany stretched to nearly four hundred pages. In both cases, the method was empirical. But the overarching narratives also suggested that revolutions could not abide compromise, and that they would either destroy those who attempted to control them or be extinguished entirely as a force of change.

Two further, very different projects from this period in Bauer's career must be considered here as well. The first was a massive series of compendia of source material from eighteenth-century authors, including a five-volume *Bibliothek der deutschen Aufklärer der achtzehnten Jahrhunderts* (which collected writings from various eighteenth-century religious reformers), and four volumes titled *Die politische Literatur der Deutschen im achtzehnten Jahrhundert* (which focused on political texts).[87] Significantly, Bauer edited this material, all of which appeared in 1846 and 1847, under the pseudonym Martin von Geismar. The second project was an extended, often poetic and sometimes satirical reflection on Bauer's experiences in prison called "Die Reise auf öffentliche Kosten." It was published in 1848 in Otto Wigand's journal *Die Epigonen*, in conjunction with the outbreak of the revolution that would also see Bauer released. The conceit of the *Bibliothek der deutschen Aufklärer* and *Die politische Literatur der Deutschen im achtzehnten Jahrhundert* was that they had been compiled by a nobleman who was attempting to prove that the Enlightenment and the

French Revolution were the consequence of Christianity, and that Christianity was a religion of slaves who had destroyed the aristocratic culture of classical antiquity. This argument was pursued most extensively in an essay called "Geschichte des Lutherthums im sechszehnten und siebzehnten Jahrhundert," which introduced the fifth volume of the *Bibliothek der deutschen Aufklärer der achtzehnten Jahrhunderts*, and which began with a speculative history of the origins of Christianity. "The Christian religion was a product of the political change that had come to light in the late Roman Empire," Bauer had von Geismar explain. In contrast with the aristocratic pagan religions of the Greeks and Romans, which expressed the values of the great noble families of those societies, "Christianity arose as the religion of the common man." This "religion of the rabble, of slaves and outcasts" was based on Judaism because the Jews were "the slaves and outcasts" of the ancient world.[88] But even after it was installed as the official religion of the Roman Empire, Bauer's alter ego proposed, it took many centuries — indeed the entire Middle Ages — before it would finally extinguish the aristocratic instinct of classical antiquity. This was the real meaning of the Reformation. And insofar as the German Enlightenment was framed by the Christian religion, insofar as it expressed itself through religious reforms, it could never retrieve the sublimity of classical antiquity.

"Die Reise auf öffentlich Kosten" or "the journey at public expense" was arguably the most interesting work that Bauer produced during the Vormärz, and it might even deserve a minor place in the great history of prison literature from Boethius and Dante to Luther and Gramsci and beyond. It had a sophisticated literary structure, and included crafted, almost Dickensian character sketches of Bauer's fellow prisoners, gripping narratives about the daily miseries of prison life, as well as comedic accounts of its unexpectedly humorous elements, long tracts of original poetry, and thoughtful philosophical treatments of topics like the virtues of solitude, the nature of the self, and the life of the mind. As a record of Bauer's political position, it was unapologetically anarchist — an earlier tendency that was fully galvanized by his time in detention. "Such are the consequences of equality before the law," Bauer wrote upon witnessing the often brutal treatment of his fellow prisoners: "The state, equally heavy on all sides with the force of a machine, has lost any organs for making distinctions. Its arms are not members of a living whole, which also have life in them and, depending on circumstances, gently rebuff, push, or bend. No. They are shovels on a locomotive that want blindly to crush the weakest and the strongest, whenever they get in its way."[89] Prison, then, revealed the true nature of the state, and the thinker who, only a handful of years earlier, had understood the republican state as the condition for genuine freedom, now saw all state forms as inescapably oppressive and carceral. The irony was that "the campaign against the state" that he had mounted in the works that had sent him to prison had been motivated by "the thought of a better, more free state" — a thought that the state had effectively beaten out of him.[90] But the destruction of that final political illusion led Bauer to a new position, in which the purpose of his criticism was no longer to change the world but to change himself: "No condition, therefore, no philosophical theory, no system of beliefs, no popular effectiveness was the result of my thinking," Bauer explained. "I myself, only I, was the goal of my development."[91]

The unmistakably Stoic pedigree of these comments was reinforced by a brilliantly paradoxical meditation on freedom, in which Bauer presented prison as both the happy realization of the apolitical life he now desired and the distilled truth of modern social existence. "The confinement of prison, which is tantamount to statelessness, suits my desires, suits the mood of my mind," Bauer wrote. "And, seen from the other direction, doesn't today's society make every place a prison for us? Doesn't it supervise our most ordinary actions, our most intimate feelings, our most passionate deeds?" But even this awareness of the modern panopticon was not enough to extinguish Bauer's Stoic resilience. Thus, Bauer insisted: "Only that is real suffering which enslaves the mind of man, drives his spirit to despair." "There is no suffering," he continued a little later, "where, in a temporary state, I see only a link in the chain of my own spiritual development. And so does prison appear to me."[92] Bauer's conclusion, which it is worth quoting at length, crystallized the argument and made it clear that the purpose of his speculations was nothing other than the creation of himself:

> And finally — the aim of criticism is not a theory that is to be put forward as the epitome of all truth — the aim of criticism is the person. It does not dwell, like a self-satisfied and sovereign power, above the critics who are its servants; no, it is nothing but the power in the mind and body of the free person. It reveals itself in the independence, the firm posture, the confident movement of this person. If, from the outset, I had only seen my dispute with the law as a personal matter, I would still have been standing on the ground of critical science. For criticism is nothing other than the science of self-liberation, and it leaves it up to each individual to decide how far he wants and can practice freedom. In reality, the matter of my science is only my own affair. As much as, in the entire attitude and motives of the judgment passed against me, in its brief and unfounded verdict, in the mere phrases that were considered sufficient, in the frenzy that resorted to comparatives and superlatives, I found proof that the law was not in a position of inviolable sovereignty, but wanted to ensure and reinforce its existence amid the feeling of being threatened, I also know that my fight against the law is a fight for my existence.[93]

In other words, for Bauer, criticism existed to strengthen the individual, and even science was ultimately a mode of self-edification. The severity of the law's persecution of Bauer was an index of its weakness, or the extent to which it felt threatened by his arguments. And his confrontation with the law was not merely juridical or even intellectual, but personal and existential.

Insurgent, Informant, Conservative

Commentators and former participants reflecting on the 1848 Revolutions in the nineteenth century often noted Bruno Bauer's conspicuously minor involvement.[94] Given his notoriety in the years leading up to the events, and his frequent calls for revolution, one might have expected him to be at the forefront. In fact, after attempting but failing to secure a seat in the Frankfurt Parliament, he participated only infrequently in public life. And he saved his most extensive comments for an analysis of the revolution's defeat, notably in his *Die bürgerliche Revolution in Deutschland* — a work that grounded the revolution in heterodox religious movements, and essentially renounced all sides in the conflict as uninspired and regressive.[95] Edgar Bauer was somewhat different. Upon his release from prison, he immediately threw himself into both practical and theoretical activity. As an example of the former, Wilhelm Piersig's *Mysterien der Berliner Demokratie* contains a harrowing (if also critical) account of Bauer leading a failed democratic insurgency on the night of August 21, 1848, when a small group of radicals backed by a large number of protesters sought to apprehend and possibly execute the liberal Minister of the Interior Friedrich von Kühlwetter and Minister of Justice Karl Anton Märker.[96] Piersig's story suggests heavily that Bauer was at the center of far-left agitation in Berlin throughout the revolution as an organizer and an activist, roughly in the conspiratorial tradition of Babeuf, Buonarroti, and Blanqui. The most obvious expression of Bauer's theoretical activity was his journal *Die Parteien: Politische Revue*, which appeared in three volumes in 1849, and which renounced efforts to establish order and stability in favor of permanent revolution.[97] "Government, democracy, socialism, citizenship," Bauer declared in the journal's first issue, "far from carrying the germ of the reorganization of society, are nothing more than the various forms in which the people's struggle for self-liberation is clothed. They have meaning," he continued, "only in strife, and strife will purify them by destroying them." Only when society abandoned all fixed political forms could it be considered free. For only then would it "no longer be held together by violence [*Gewalt*], but by the determination, the insight, the desire to work [*Arbeitslust*] and the constantly changing interest of the people."[98]

Bauer's movements in the years following the revolution become more difficult to trace, as, like so many European radicals, he was forced to flee the reaction that took hold. But a considerable amount of archival research on this period was conducted in the 1980s by the German Democratic Republic scholar Eric Gamby.[99] On Gamby's account, Bauer left Berlin in 1849, shortly after Friedrich Wilhelm IV's troops reentered the city unopposed. At first, he lived in Hamburg under a false name. He then moved to Altona in Denmark, where he worked as an editor for the *Norddeutschen Freien Presse* and the *Altonaer Zeitung*. When the newly restored regime in Prussia demanded his extradition in 1851, he relied on the assistance of the philologist and art historian Peder Hjort and the Danish police commissioner Cosmus Braestrup to escape with his family to London. The following year, Braestrup traveled to London and met with Bauer. And that appears to be the moment when Bauer was recruited as a spy for the Danish government, commissioned with the task of reporting on the large community of European exiles and former revolutionaries living in the city. Bauer's first report for Braestrup was completed on November 7, 1852, and included detailed information on the activities of Arnold Ruge and former contributors to Ruge's *Jahrbücher* (including Marx and Engels) as well as their French and Italian contacts. Four more reports on German revolutionaries and their international associates were delivered by Bauer between 1852 and 1853, followed by shorter ones that lasted until 1861. These documents, which remained secret until 1899, appear to have been highly valued, and were circulated among police throughout Europe. They also served as Bauer's primary source of income. And when the Danish government decided that they were no longer required, his living conditions deteriorated considerably.[100]

While he was never as influential as he had been during the 1840s, Bauer continued to work as a writer throughout the rest of his life. The record suggests that, over time, he took a slow but inexorable shift to the right, as the disillusioned democrat transformed into a hardened conservative. For example, Bauer's *Englische Freiheit*, which was published by Otto Wigand in 1857, consisted of a series of journalistic dispatches written between January 1856 and January 1857 on the political events of the day, notably the Crimean War, the Chartist movement, and the statesmanship and diplomacy of figures like Richard Cobden and Lord Palmerston. And it basically argued that England was the most advanced nation in Europe. "England maintains its hegemony," Bauer claimed, "because on its soil the answers to the great questions that determine the fate of civil society are taking place. England fights the battle between capital and labor, in England one learns how parties arise, combine, and die, England develops the forms of dictatorship and parliamentarism, England shows how strict ecclesiasticism and toleration can go hand in hand, England reveals the mysteries of humanity."[101] *Reflections on the Integrity of the Danish Monarchy* and *Schleswig* were shorter pamphlets that Bauer wrote in English in 1857 and 1861 respectively. They both took the side of the Danish monarchy against the German nationalists in the Schleswig-Holstein dispute of the mid-nineteenth century. And they suggested that, along with his work as a spy, Bauer had taken on the role of propagandist for the Danish government. When he returned to Germany following the 1861 amnesty for the 1848 revolutionaries, Bauer continued the same propaganda project in works like his 1863 *Das Herzogthum Holstein und seine Rechte* and his 1873 *Artikel V, der deutsche Gedanke und die dänische Monarchie*. In 1871, under the patronage of the orthodox Bishop of Holstein Wilhelm Heinrich Koopmann, he became editor of the conservative *Kirchliche Blatter*.

During this final stage in his career, Bauer also wrote, among other things, a curious history of Freemasonry titled *Freimaurer Bund und das Licht*, another study of similar secret societies called *Zwei Ordensskizzen*, and the novella *Der Magus des Nordens* (which claimed to be written by Dr. Edgar Bauer even though Bauer was not a doctor). But in terms of their scholarly significance, two of Bauer's late works probably deserve more attention than I can offer here: his 1872 *Die Wahrheit über die Internationale* (which was a critical response to Marx's discussion of the Paris Commune in *The Civil War in France*); and his 1884 *Das Capital und die Capitalmacht* (which was also written partly in response to Marx, and which treated capitalism as a cultural and historical rather than narrowly economic phenomenon). In the first of these, Bauer proposed that the international revolutionary movement that had revealed itself so dramatically during the Paris Commune of 1871 had its roots in London's émigré community, especially in the organizations designed by Arnold Ruge, Giuseppe Mazzini, and Alexandre Ledru-Rollin following the 1848 Revolutions. Marx's contribution had been to claim this movement in the name of the proletariat or the urban working class. In effect, Bauer argued that both sides of the class war that Marx had repeatedly promoted — both the bourgeoisie and the proletariat — advanced the same spiritually empty ethic of impersonal interest. The concrete expression of this ethic, Bauer proposed, was the stock market, which privileged the circulation of capital over individuals, and transformed the struggle of workers with identifiable capitalists into a struggle with abstract economic corporations. Indeed, as Bauer saw it, the collectively owned corporation of the stock market neatly reflected the collective economic social body that the communists wanted to create. The general drift of modernity was thus away from authentic individuality and toward a mindless mass. And if successful, Bauer predicted, "the worker will have to bear the heavy consequences of his victory over personal property, just as the people are haunted by their triumph over the individual princes."[102]

Das Capital und die Capitalmacht located the origin of capital in the ancient world, and specifically in ancient Rome, when the landed property of the Roman nobility was combined with the monetary wealth of the Sabine tribe, after the Romans had abducted the Sabinean women as wives. Roman law was designed to protect this new form of combined wealth. Bauer went on to provide a genealogy for the origins of money and property in the ancient world, arguing that the initial form of wealth was the gift, and that private property emerged slowly out of a more original communal ownership. He then projected forward from the ancient world to the Middle Ages, when the church sought to comprehend property within the legal apparatus of the feudal system, and early modernity, when the expansion of conquest and trade strengthened the corporations and the banks to the point where, in the seventeenth century, the economic power of capital trumped the political power of the state. "In political terms," Bauer wrote, "this sentence is written at the gate of the new era: 'The condition of economic life is freedom, and the task of state power is only to guarantee this freedom in the name of public welfare.'"[103] The emergence of modern science, including political economy, was part of an effort to reassert the authority of reason and the state. Elements of the French Revolution also resisted capital, but ultimately, with Napoleon and the Civil Code, it further entrenched its legal justification. The nineteenth century saw the rise of socialism, from the French utopians Charles Fourier and Saint Simon to "two important geniuses of the Hegel school Ferdinand Lassalle and Karl Marx,"[104] the latter of whom Bauer praised as "the great spirit of social democracy" and "the real, perhaps the last student of Hegel."[105] But ultimately, Bauer concluded, socialism was a destructive force. For the revolution it fomented effectively reinforced the system it claimed to fight, and only a monarchy or "dynasty" could place substantive legal limits on property.[106]

Anarchist Philosophy and Instituent Power

After being paralyzed by a stroke in 1884, Bauer died of a heart attack in Hanover on August 18, 1886. Already during his lifetime, he had garnered enough notoriety to be mentioned in histories of German literature and popular encyclopedias.[107] But subsequent scholarship has been piecemeal. In the early twentieth century, the anarchist historian Max Nettlau claimed him as an important precursor to the anarchist movement, and even represented him, along with Max Stirner, as one of its founders.[108] Around the same time, the social democratic scholar Gustav Meyer assigned him a key role in the history of radicalism and characterized him as a critic of liberal constitutionalism and proponent of unrestricted democracy.[109] Throughout the twentieth century, the reception of all the Young Hegelians, Bauer included, was in many ways drowned out by the publication of scholarly editions of Marx's and Engels's polemics against them in *The Holy Family* and *The German Ideology*. The first (and as far as I know only) person to work systematically through Bauer's literary remains was Eric Gamby, who, as mentioned above, was particularly interested in his work as a spy and his documentation of the activities of European exiles in London, including Marx and other important figures in the history of the workers' movement. In the English-speaking world, intellectual historians like Lawrence Stepelevich and Eric V. Luft provided brief accounts of Bauer's thought, focusing on the vehemence of his calls for revolution, up to and including revolutionary terror. Roughly the same approach was taken by Ingrid Pepperle.[110] But the most sophisticated interpretation of Bauer's political views was that of Wolfgang Eßbach, whose seminal work on the Young Hegelians in the late 1980s proposed that Bauer was far more innovative than Marx and Engels allowed, and even the likely source of some of the ideas for which Marx is still typically credited. Indeed, and as noted above, Eßbach went so far as to claim that elements of Marx's mature approach to politics could be attributed to his reading of Bauer's *Der Streit der Kritik mit Kirche und Staat* and its elaboration of an "anti-utopian social revolutionary anarchism that relies on the proletariat and that seeks to define its relevant movement beyond the form of the political party."[111]

But it would be a mistake to finish this study with the suggestion that Bauer's thought is of exclusively historical interest, and particularly that its value is determined by its influence on Marx. For his work speaks to contemporary political theorists as well. Here I will conclude with two brief examples, both of which could be supplemented with many more: Catherine Malabou's *Stop Thief! Anarchism and Philosophy*, which appeared in the French original and English translation in 2023; and Roberto Esposito's *Institution*, which was published in Italian in 2021 and translated into English in 2022. Malabou began her career in the 1990s with a transformative interpretation of Hegel that presented him, not as a dangerous theorist of "totality" (which is how he had been characterized in much twentieth-century continental philosophy), but as a thinker of plasticity, futurity, and the event of reading.[112] In *Stop Thief!* she argues that we are currently facing a "crisis of horizontality" as movements on the right have appropriated much of the anarchistic rhetoric that once belonged to the left, making it necessary to reinvent our political idiom. However, she maintains, philosophy offers little assistance in this regard. For even contemporary philosophies that affirm anarchy at a conceptual level (including the work of Levinas, Foucault, Derrida, Agamben, and Rancière) never affirm anarch*ism* at the political one. On Malabou's account, therefore, the immediate task is to dismantle the link between philosophy, on one side, and the logic of government, on the other.[113] Here I will only say that a figure like Bauer answers Malabou's challenge well, and that it can hardly be accidental that he also emerges out of a deep engagement with Hegel (the great philosopher of the state) into anarchism. Indeed, Bauer's later anarchist position can only be understood as a consistent application of his earlier one — a philosophy built out of a Hegelian or even Hegelo–Malabouvian response to the contingency of events.

From something like the opposite direction, Esposito claims that the left has an inadequate relationship with institutions that, following the approach set down by Marx and Engels, it has generally treated in instrumental and epiphenomenal terms, as tools in the hands of powerful interests or secondary expressions of a material base. However, as the COVID-19 pandemic revealed in particularly stark terms, this set of assumptions is no longer adequate to our political experience, especially at a moment when the right has developed a successful anti-institutional rhetoric of its own. Beginning with the obscure Roman legal expression *vitam instituere* or "to institute life," then, Esposito suggests we conceive of institutions, not as static forms, but as dynamic processes or manifestations of a vital, biopolitical force he calls "instituent power," which he distinguishes from a post-Heideggerian "distituent power," on the one hand, and the Spinozist–Deleuzian version of "constituent power," on the other.

Neither purely negative nor purely affirmative (but also not a dialectic between the two), this instituent power would pursue order through conflict. Or, put differently, it would give political and symbolic shape to the instituting force of conflict, while at the same time dismantling any instituted form.[114] Here again a closer study of Bauer and his contemporaries would contribute to the agenda. For, as I have emphasized throughout this work, the Young Hegelians were precisely institutional warriors seeking to revolutionize the Prussian state through complex but effective theoretical struggles. And their failure and disillusion with this model seeded the theory of the state, the law, and institutions more generally that took shape in Marx's and Engels's later work and that in many ways generated the lacunae that Esposito's most recent writings are designed to redress. In either case, if our aim is "to institute life" we could do worse than to study the Young Hegelian struggle to secularize and render fully human the mystical institutions of the Prussian state and church.

Perhaps the most striking detail about Edgar Bauer's career is how young he was when he produced his major works. He was born in 1820, meaning that the decade before and during the 1848 Revolutions corresponded with his twenties. And, for better and for worse, his work from that period is marked by a youthful enthusiasm that is surely familiar to anyone who was politically active at an early age. But that should not be grounds for diminishing its significance. Indeed, the politics of any time would be much less vibrant without the rash and reckless affect manifest in figures like Edgar Bauer. We know only a little bit about the way others in Bauer's immediate circle perceived him during his life, and what we do know suggests that he was roguish in a manner that some found off-putting. A letter from Jenny Marx to Engels from around August 14, 1857, recounts one of Bauer's visits to the Marx household in London. "A few evenings ago, that clown Edgar Bauer came to see us," Jenny contemptuously writes. "Truly a dried cod — without any cod-liver oil and on top of that with pretensions to wit. So frightful were his efforts that I almost fainted, while Karl was sick — not just figuratively but in fact."[115] More intriguing still, particularly given its connection to *Es leben feste Grundsätze!* is an anecdote from the communist typesetter and revolutionary Stephan Born's memoir *Erinnerungen eines Achtundvierzigers*:

> At the beginning of the 1840s, Edgar Bauer published a volume of novellas together with the Alsatian Alexandre Weill, who was visiting Berlin at the time. They were printed by my master, so I had to bring the corrections to Bauer several times. As soon as I entered the room, I was struck by the obscene lithographs he had posted on the wall. The conversation he started with me while I was reading the proof also had a disgusting character. From then on, I developed an insurmountable antipathy toward the man, who, I later found out, had sunk into a swamp.[116]

As we have seen, while Bauer did not exactly sink into a swamp, he was certainly a great deal less influential — and less inventive — following the 1848 Revolutions than he was before them. But for a brief moment during the 1840s, he was unquestionably the most outspoken revolutionary in German letters, and the one most willing to accept the consequences of a line of thought that others only followed to the place where it became uncomfortable. And anyone who wants to understand such extremism — which will never be eliminated from public life altogether and might even form an essential aspect of politics as such — can only claim to have done so with at least some exposure to his thinking and his life.

Notes

Preface

1. For contemporary accounts of these events, see: Friedrich Sass, *Berlin in seiner neuesten Zeit und Entwicklung* (Leipzig: Koffka, 1846), 162–78; Robert Pruß, *Vorlesungen über die deutsche Literatur der Gegenwart* (Leipzig: Mayer, 1847), 329–40; Julian Schmidt, *Geschichte der deutschen Literatur im neunzehnten Jahrhundert. Dritter Band. Die Gegenwart* (Leipzig: Herbig, 1855), 405–29; Robert Pruß, *Zehn Jahre. Geschichte der neuesten Zeit. 1840–1850. Zweiter Band* (Leipzig: Weber, 1856), 388–93. See also: Wolfgang Eßbach, *Die Junghegelianer: Soziologie einer Intellektuellengruppe* (München: Wilhelm Fink, 1988), 176–225.

2. See: Anonymous, "Literarisches Forum. Berliner Novellen. Von A. Weill und Edgar Bauer. Berlin, Berliner Verlagshandlung. 1843," in *Berliner Wespen. Fünftes Heft*, ed. Feodor Wehl (Leipzig: Recalm, 1843), 42–44; Anonymous, "Novellen. 1. Berliner Novellen. Von A. Weill und Edgar Bauer. Berliner Verlagsbuchhandlung. 1843," *Literaturblatt* 115 (November 10, 1843): 460; Anonymous, "Unterhaltungsliteratur. 1. Berliner Novellen. Von A. Weill und Edgar Bauer. Berlin, Berliner Verlagsbuchhandlung. 1843," *Blätter für literarische Unterhaltung* 146 (May 25, 1844), 583.

3. For older studies of the Young Hegelians, see: Sidney Hook, *From Hegel to Marx: Studies in the Intellectual Development of Karl Marx* (New York: John Day, 1936); David McLellan, *The Young Hegelians and Karl Marx* (London: Praeger, 1969); Harold Mah, *The End of Philosophy and the Origin of Ideology: Karl Marx and the Crisis of the Young Hegelians* (Berkeley: University of California Press, 1987). More recent scholarship includes: Warren Breckman, *Marx, the Young Hegelians, and the Origins of Radical Social Theory: Dethroning the Self* (Cambridge: Cambridge University Press, 1999); Douglas Moggach, *The Philosophy and Politics of Bruno Bauer* (Cambridge: Cambridge University Press, 2003); Douglas Moggach, ed., *The New Hegelians: Philosophy and Politics in the Hegelian School* (Cambridge: Cambridge University Press, 2006); Lars Lambrecht, ed., *"Umstürzende Gedanken": Radikale Theorie im Vorfeld der 1848er Revolution* (Frankfurt am Main: Peter Lang, 2013); Michael Quante and Amir Mohseni, eds., *Die linken Hegelianer: Studien zum Verhältnis von Religion und Politik im Vormärz* (Leiden: Brill, 2015).

4. The established literature on Edgar Bauer is limited. Nothing like a history of interpretation exists. The most systematic account of his career to date is: Erik Gamby, *Edgar Bauer: Junghegelianer, Publizist, und Polizeiagent, mit Bibliographie der E. Bauer. Texte und Dokumentenanhang* (Trier: Karl-Marx-Haus, 1985). See also: Eric V. Luft, "Edgar Bauer and the Origins of the Theory of Terrorism," in *The New Hegelians: Politics and Philosophy in the Hegelian School*, ed. Douglas Moggach (Cambridge:

Cambridge University Press, 2006); Charles Barbour, "'The True Practice is Theory': Edgar Bauer, Republicanism, and the Young Hegelians," *International Critical Thought* 12, no. 4 (2022): 640–60.

5. Herbert De Vriese, "Not a Man of Solid Principles: The Relevance of Edgar Bauer's Polemical Portrait of Karl Marx in His 1843 Novella *Es leben feste Grundsätze!*," *European Journal of the History of Economic Thought* 25, no. 5 (2018): 679–709.

6. On Young Hegelianism and republicanism, see: Douglas Moggach, *The Philosophy and Politics of Bruno Bauer* (Cambridge: Cambridge University Press, 2005); Gareth Stedman Jones, "The Young Hegelians, Marx and Engels," in *The Cambridge History of Nineteenth-Century Political Thought*, ed. Gareth Stedman Jones and Gregory Claeys (Cambridge: Cambridge University Press, 2011), 556–600; Bruno Leipold, *Citizen Marx: Republicanism and the Formation of Karl Marx's Social and Political Thought* (Princeton: Princeton University Press, 2024). Among many others, the best examples of the Young Hegelian appropriation of Hegel's political theory are: Arnold Ruge, "Zur Kritik des gegenwartigen Staats- und Völkerrechts," *Hallische Jahrbücher für deutsche Wissenschaft und Kunst* 151–56 (June 24–30, 1840): 1201–43; Arnold Ruge, "Die Hegelsche Rechtsphilosophie und die Politik unserer Zeit," *Deutsche Jahrbücher für Wissenschaft und Kunst* 189–92 (August 10–13, 1842): 755–68.

7. Henry Vizetelly, *Berlin Under the New Empire, Volume 1* (London: Tinsley Brothers, 1879), 57–60; Ernst Dronke, *Berlin, Zweiter Band* (Frankfurt am Main: Literarische Anstalt, 1846), 29–70.

8. Ernst Dronke, *Berlin, Erster Band* (Frankfurt am Main: Literarische Anstalt, 1846); Dronke, *Berlin, Zweiter Band*; Friedrich Sass, *Berlin in seiner neuesten Zeit und Entwicklung*; Anonymous, *Die Geheimnisse von Berlin: Aus den Papieren eines Berliner Kriminalbeamten* (Berlin: Meyer und Hoffman, 1844).

9. Arnold Ruge and Theodore Echtermeyer, "Die Protestantismus und die Romantik," *Hallische Jahrbücher für deutsche Wissenschaft und Kunst* 245–51, 265–71, 53–64 (1838, 1839): 2113–64, 2401–80, 417–512; Schmidt, *Geschichte der deutschen Literatur*, 405–08; Peter Uwe Hohendahl, "Literary Criticism in the Epoch of Liberalism, 1820–70," in *A History of German Literary Criticism, 1780–1980*, ed. Peter Uwe Hohendahl (Lincoln: University of Nebraska Press, 1988), 239–55.

Part One

1. The Spree is the river that runs through Berlin. It is relatively shallow and unnavigable by large ships. There is probably a slanted reference here to Heinrich Heine's satirical poem "Peace." "And the patient water of the sacred Spree, / Washes souls and dilutes the tea [*Die Seelen wäscht und den Thee verdünnt*]." Heinrich Heine, "Peace," *The Poems of Heinrich Heine*, trans. Edgar Alfred Bowring (London: Bell and Daldy, 1866), 250.

2. The dog tax was a luxury tax imposed on dog owners. Versions of the tax dated back to the Middle Ages. On April 29, 1829, Friedrich Wilhelm III issued a Cabinet Order that

shifted the authority to collect the tax to the municipalities, where it was used to generate revenue for city planning and improvement.

3. Diogenes the Cynic (412 or 404–323 BCE) was an ancient Greek philosopher who flouted the hypocritical norms of Greek society. According to Diogenes Laertius, his search for an honest man involved holding a lantern up to the faces of his fellow citizens in broad daylight.

4. *Botokuden* was common nineteenth-century slang for an uncivilized place. The word was derived from the Portuguese name for certain indigenous tribes of Brazil, or *Botocudo* (from *botoque* or plug, which referred to the ornaments some wore in their lips and ears).

5. Kreuzberg is a district of Berlin. During the 1840s, it was essentially pastoral farmland. Here the narrator is ironically contrasting it with the more menacing natural environments — notably forests — that often figured in Romantic novels.

6. Passion painters or *Passionsmaler* refers to extravagant artistic depictions of the events of Christ's trial, crucifixion, and resurrection. The narrator's point is that he does not intend to exaggerate for emotional effect.

7. The Battle of Jena (October 14, 1806) marked the humiliating defeat of the Prussian Army at the hands of Napoleon's forces. As a result, Prussia was reduced to a vassal state until the Wars of Liberation (1813–14), which generated a powerful nationalist fervor roughly coincident with the rise of German Romanticism.

8. The reference is to the 1830 July Revolution in France, in which the regime of the Bourbon King Charles X was overturned and replaced by a constitutional monarchy under his cousin Louis Phillipe. The events of the July Revolution sent shock waves throughout Europe and galvanized the political positions of both its conservative opponents and its liberal supporters.

9. In 1840 Prussian King Friedrich Wilhelm III died and his son Friedrich Wilhelm IV ascended to the throne. Liberals saw this as an opportunity to demand the new king keep his father's 1815 promise to grant Prussian citizens a representative constitution. Initially, it seemed as if Friedrich Wilhelm IV might adopt liberal policies. But his regime quickly took a conservative turn and moved to suppress constitutionalism. "Young screaming-souls" refers to radical journalists and "old scribing-souls" to obedient bureaucrats.

10. Joseph, Duke of Saxe-Altenburg (1789–1868) ruled Saxe-Altenburg, one of Germany's smallest states, from 1834 to 1848. He was deeply conservative and resistant to reform. Ludwig I of Bavaria (1786–1868) reigned over the predominantly Catholic Kingdom of Bavaria from 1825 to 1848. While he initially introduced liberal reforms, he became increasingly conservative following the 1830 July Revolution in France. In the nineteenth century Charlottenburg was a municipality to the west of Berlin known primarily for Charlottenburg Palace, the preferred residence of numerous Prussian kings. Originally components of the complex constitutional arrangements of the Holy Roman Empire, free imperial cities were cities that possessed a measure of governmental autonomy.

11. The *Allgemeine preußische Staats-zeitung* was the official journal of the Prussian government. It was known for its lack of editorial independence and its extensive presentation of statistical information void of commentary or opinion.

12. Arthur is inventing an insulting name for one of his noble acquaintances. *Sonderling* — a diminutive of *sonder* or special — is German slang meaning strange, eccentric, or odd.

13. The *Rheinische Zeitung für Politik, Handel und Gewerbe* was one of the most outspoken newspapers of the period. It was designed to promote the agenda of Rhineland liberals. In particular, it lobbied for a Prussian constitution and a representative National Assembly. But it also became a platform for more radical projects. It first appeared in January 1842 and was finally suppressed in April 1843. From October 1842 to March 1843, it was edited by Karl Marx. Many of the Young Hegelians, including Edgar Bauer, were frequent contributors.

14. On January 31, 1843, Friedrich Wilhelm IV issued a Cabinet Order that rescinded the more liberal approach to censorship that had been announced by a Cabinet Order on December 10, 1842. On February 4, 1843, that Cabinet Order was reinforced by a Censorship Instruction that installed a new *Ober Censurgericht* or Higher Censorship Court with the power to impose long prison sentences on offenders. This heavy-handed approach to censorship effectively destroyed the radical press and the Young Hegelian movement.

15. The Order of the Red Eagle was an honor awarded by Prussian monarchs to Prussian citizens in recognition of either military or civil service. It included first through fourth classes, as well as a dizzying array of variations within each class. Here it is indicative of the privy councillor's careerism and steadfast commitment to the dominant order.

16. Many of the Young Hegelian books and pamphlets (including works by Arnold Ruge, Ludwig Feuerbach, Max Stirner, Friedrich Engels, Bruno Bauer, and Edgar Bauer) were published in Leipzig by the bookseller Otto Wigand. Leipzig was in Saxony, which from 1830 had a liberal constitution and more lenient censorship laws than neighboring Prussia.

17. Karl is invoking the familiar story, first recounted by Plutarch, that the ancient Spartans either executed or abandoned newborn children deemed physically inferior.

18. Familius Wagner is a character in Johann Wolfgang Goethe's *Faust, a Tragedy*. He is generally understood to represent the complacency that results from excessive faith in the power of reason and progress.

19. In Greek mythology, Actaeon is a hunter who stumbles across the goddess Artemis while she is bathing naked. As punishment, Artemis has him transformed into a stag and hunted by his own dogs. The story of Pyramus and Thisbe is from Ovid's *Metamorphoses*. In it, Pyramus mistakenly believes Thisbe has been killed by a lion and commits suicide in despair.

20. The Leipzig Fair or Leipziger Messe was a large trade fair and public market held multiple times a year in the city of Leipzig dating back to the twelfth century.

21. The reference is to Friedrich Schiller's popular play *The Robbers*, which tells the story of the rebellious Karl Moor and his scheming brother Franz. It is invoked here to suggest that Baron Arthur may have been idealistic and philosophical in his youth.

22. The court councillor refers to the Hungarian composer and piano virtuoso Franz Liszt (1811–1886), the German author and critic Johann Wolfgang Goethe (1749–1832), and the celebrated nineteenth-century soprano Sophie Löwe (1815–1866).

Part Two

1. The first half of the nineteenth century saw the emergence and proliferation of a large number of temperance societies or *Mäßigkeitsvereine*. This was partly in response to a shift in drinking habits, particularly among the poor, when German distilleries began using potatoes rather than grains to produce alcohol, flooding the market with potent schnapps as opposed to beer.

2. Albert is playing on the German idiom for a hangover or *katzenjammer*, which roughly translates as "cat's grief."

3. Jakob Böhme (1575-1624) was a German philosopher and mystic with a profound influence on subsequent schools of thought, notably German Idealism and Romanticism. Hans Sachs (1494–1576) was a shoemaker who became a famous singer and poet. He is remembered for, among other things, his ardent support for Luther and the Reformation.

4. Kreuzberg is a small hill in Berlin that gives the Kreuzberg neighborhood its name. Vesuvius is the Italian volcano that famously erupted in 79 CE and destroyed the city of Pompeii.

5. Prussian censorship laws required that books up to twenty sheets (roughly 160 pages) be censored prior to publication. Larger works were exempt. The rationale was that, while the law was intended to control information circulating among the general population, larger works were designed for specialist audiences. Thus, in principle, the censorship would not interfere with the advance of science.

6. The Latin *indicium* means index or sign. By "police indicium" the captain means something like "a mere clue" — a single piece of evidence but not an entire case.

Afterword

1. Edgar Bauer and Friedrich Engels [Anonymous], *Die frech bedräute, jedoch wunderbar befreite Bibel, oder, Der Triumph des Glaubens* (Neumünster bei Zürich: Heß, 1842), 27.

2. Edgar Bauer, *Bruno Bauer und seine Gegner* (Berlin: Jonas, 1842), 37.

3. Edgar Bauer, *Die liberalen Bestrebungen in Deutschland, Erstes Heft: Die Ostpreußische Opposition in Deutschland* (Zurich und Winterthur: Literaischen Comptoirs, 1843), 27.

4. Edgar Bauer, *Die liberalen Bestrebungen, Erstes Heft*, 58.

5. Edgar Bauer [Anonymous], "Vörlaufiges über Bruno Bauer, Kritik der evangelischen Geschichte der Synoptiker," *Deutsche Jahrbücher für Wissenschaft und Kunst*, no. 105 (1842): 417–18.

6. Eric Gamby, "Einführung," in *Konfidentenberichte über die europäische Emigration in London 1852–1861*, ed. Eric Gamby (Trier: Karl-Marx-Haus, 1989), xi–xviii.

7. Quentin Skinner, *Visions of Politics*, vol. 1, *Regarding Method* (Cambridge: Cambridge University Press, 2002).

8. Bruno Bauer, *Kritik der Geschichte der Offenbarung. Die Religion des Alten Testamentes in der geschichtlichen Entwickelung ihrer Principien dargestellt, Erster Band* (Berlin: Dümmler, 1838), xv–c.

9. David Strauss, *Streitschriften zur vertheidigung meiner schrift über das Leben Jesu, Drittes Heft* (Tübingen: Osiender, 1837), 95–120.

10. Bruno Bauer, "Das Leben Jesu, kritisch bearbeiten, Erster Band," *Jahrbücher für wissenschaftliche Kritik* 109–13 (1837): 879–912; Bruno Bauer, "Das Leben Jesu, kritisch bearbeiten, Zweiter Band," *Jahrbücher für wissenschaftliche Kritik* 86–88 (1836): 681–704; Bruno Bauer, "Schriften über Strauss Leben Jesu." *Jahrbücher für wissenschaftliche Kritik* 41–43 (1837): 321–40.

11. Douglas Moggach, *The Philosophy and Politics of Bruno Bauer* (Cambridge: Cambridge University Press, 2003). See also: Charles Barbour, "The Political Theology and Polemical Tactics of Bruno Bauer," *The European Legacy* 29, no. 2 (2024): 143–65.

12. Robert M. Bigler, *The Politics of German Protestantism* (Berkeley: University of California Press, 1972), 38–52; Christopher Clark, "Confessional Policy and the Limits of State Action: Frederick William III and the Prussian Church Union 1817–40," *Historical Journal* 39, no. 4 (December 1996): 985–1004; Christopher Clark, *Iron Kingdom: The Rise and Downfall of Prussia, 1600–1947* (Cambridge, MA: Belknap Press, 2006), 415–19.

13. Bruno Bauer, *Die evangelische Landeskirche Preussens und die Wissenschaft* (Leipzig: Wigand, 1840), 36.

14. Bruno Bauer, *Die evangelische Landeskirche*, 60.

15. Christopher Clark, "Religion," in *Germany 1800–1870*, ed. Jonathan Sperber (Oxford: Oxford University Press, 2004), 162–84; Christopher Clark, "Germany 1815–1848: Restoration or Pre-March?," in *Nineteenth-Century Germany: Politics, Culture and Society, 1780–1918*, ed. John Breuilly (London: Bloomsbury, 2001). Clark maintains that "the dynamism of religion as an autonomous social force was arguably greater during this era than at any time since the late seventeenth century" (44–45). See also: John E. Toews, "Church and State," in *The Cambridge History of Nineteenth-Century Political Thought*, ed. Gareth Stedman Jones and Gregory Claeys (Cambridge: Cambridge University Press, 2011), 603–48.

16. Bruno Bauer, *Kritik der evangelischen Geschichte der Synoptiker, Erster Band* (Leipzig: Wigand, 1842), v–xxiv.

17. A record of the investigation and its findings was published as: Evangelisch-theologischen Facultät der Rheinischen Friedrich-Wilhelms-Universität, *Gutachten der Evangelisch theologischen Facultäten der Königlich Preußischen Universitäten über den Licentiaten Bruno Bauer in Beziehung auf dessen Kritik der evangelischen Geschichte der Synoptiker* (Berlin: Dümmler, 1842). For a generous contemporary account of Bauer's dismissal, see: Anonymous, "Preußen seit der Einfeßung Arndt's bis zur Abfeßung Bauers," in *Einundzwanzig Bogen aus der Schweiz*, ed. Georg Herwegh (Zürich und Winterthur: Literarischen Comptoirs, 1843), 26–32. For a critical account, see: Karl Hermann Scheidler [Anonymous], "Beitrag zur Verständigung über Begriff und Wesen, Nothwendigkeit und Schranken der theologischen Lehrfreiheit (mit Beziehung auf den Bruno Bauer'schen Fall)," in Minerva, Zweiter Band, ed. Friedrich Bran (Jena: Bran, 1842), 321–59.

18. Bruno Bauer, *Die gute Sache der Frieheit und meine eigene Angelegenheit* (Zürich und Winterthur: Literarischen Comptoirs, 1842), 33.

19. Four of Edgar Bauer's reviews in the *Deutsche Jahrbücher* form the backbone of *Bruno Bauer und Seine Gegner*: Edgar Bauer [Dr. Radge], "Die Bruno Bauersche Angelegenheit. Einleitung in die öffentlichen Vorlesungen über die Bedeutung der Hegelschen Philosophie in der christlichen Theologie. Nebst einem Separatvotum über B. Bauer's Kritik der evangelischen Geschichte. Von Dr. Philipp Marheineke. Berlin 1842," *Deutsche Jahrbücher für Wissenschaft und Kunst* 151–54 (June 27–30, 1842): 601–15; Edgar Bauer [Dr. Radge], "Bruno Bauer und die akademische Lehrfreiheit von Dr. O. F. Gruppe. Berlin 1842. Albert Nauck," *Deutsche Jahrbücher für Wissenschaft und Kunst* 173–75 (July 22–25, 1842): 692–98; Edgar Bauer [B. Radge], "Ueber die Anstellung der Theologen an den deutschen Universitäten. Theologisches Votum. Berlin 1842. Berliner Lesecabinet," *Deutsche Jahrbücher für Wissenschaft und Kunst* 187–89 (August 8–10, 1842): 745–55; Edgar Bauer [Dr. Radge], "Protestantische Lehrfreiheit. 1) Minerva, Maiheft 1842. Beitrag zur Verständigung über Begriff und Wesen Nothwendigkeit und Schranken der theologischen Lehrfreiheit. Mit Beziehung auf den Bruno Bauerschen Fall. 2) Bauer und die protestantische Lehrfreiheit, ein politisches Votum," *Deutsche Jahrbücher für Wissenschaft und Kunst* 225–27 (September 21–23, 1842): 897–907.

20. Edgar Bauer, *Bruno Bauer*, 4–5.

21. Edgar Bauer, *Bruno Bauer*, 7.

22. Edgar Bauer, *Bruno Bauer*, 8.

23. Edgar Bauer, *Bruno Bauer*, 27.

24. For examples of contemporaries of the Young Hegelians making this accusation, see: Ernst Hengstenberg, "Die Vollbrachte Revolution," *Evangelische Kirchenzeitung* 57 (1842): 449–51; Karl Biedermann, *Die deutsche Philosophie vom Kant bis unsre Zeit, Zweiter Band* (Leipzig: Meyer und Wigand, 1842), 514; Karl Hermann Schiedler, "Hegel (Neuhegelianer)," in *Das Staats-Lexikon, Sechster Band*, ed. Carl Rotteck and Carl Welcker (Altona: Hammerich, 1847), 629–63. See also: Charles Barbour, "A

Liberal Before Liberalism: Karl Hermann Scheidler and the New Hegelians," *Modern Intellectual History* 18 (2021): 658–80.

25. Edgar Bauer, *Bruno Bauer*, 104.

26. Edgar Bauer, *Bruno Bauer*, 105.

27. For an example of the former, see: Otto Friedrich Gruppe, *Bruno Bauer und die akademische Lehrfreiheit* (Berlin: Rauck, 1842). For the latter, see: Philipp Konrad Marheineke, *Einleitung in die öffentlichen Vorlesungen über die Bedeutung der Hegelschen Philosophie in der christlichen Theologie, Nebst einem Separatvotum über B. Bauers Kritik der evangelischen Geschichte* (Berlin: Enslin, 1842).

28. Edgar Bauer, *Bruno Bauer*, 89.

29. Edgar Bauer, *Bruno Bauer*, 90.

30. Edgar Bauer, *Bruno Bauer*, 92.

31. Edgar Bauer, *Bruno Bauer*, 94.

32. Edgar Bauer, *Bruno Bauer*, 106.

33. Edgar Bauer, "Geschichte Europa's seit der ersten französischen Revolution von Archibald Alison, deutsch von Dr. Ludwig Meyer. Erster und zweiter Band. Leipzig 1842. Otto Wigand," *Deutsche Jahrbücher für Wissenschaft und Kunst* 297–99 (December 14–16, 1842): 1185.

34. Edgar Bauer, "Geschichte Europa's seit der ersten französischen Revolution," 1186.

35. Edgar Bauer, "Geschichte Europa's seit der ersten französischen Revolution," 1195.

36. On the complex meanings of the term *liberal* in nineteenth-century political discourse, see: Jörn Leonhard, "Formulating and Reformulating 'Liberalism,'" in *In Search of European Liberalisms: Concepts, Languages, Ideologies*, eds Fernández-Sebastián Freeden and Jörn Leonhard (Oxford: Oxford University Press, 2019), 72–101; Charles Barbour, "Partisan of the Absolute State: Arnold Ruge, Liberalism, and the *Hallische Jahrbücher*," *Central European History* (first view). See also: James J. Sheehan, *German Liberalism in the Nineteenth Century* (Chicago: University of Chicago Press, 1978), 7–78; David F. Lindenfeld, *The Practical Imagination: The German Sciences of State in the Nineteenth Century* (Chicago: University of Chicago Press, 1997), 89–157; Michael Stolleis, *Public Law in Germany: A Historical Introduction from the 16th to the 21st Century*, trans. Thomas Dunlap (Oxford: Oxford University Press, 2017), 115–37; Wolfgang J. Mommsen, "German Liberalism in the Nineteenth Century," in *The Cambridge History of Nineteenth-Century Political Thought*, ed. Gareth Stedman Jones and Gregory Claeys (Cambridge: Cambridge University Press, 2011), 409–32; Jerrold Seigel, "European Liberalism in the Nineteenth Century," in *The Cambridge History of Modern European Thought*, ed. Warren Breckman and Peter E. Gordon (Cambridge: Cambridge University Press, 2019), 172–95.

37. Edgar Bauer and Bruno Bauer, *Briefwechsel zwischen Bruno Bauer und Edgar Bauer während der Jahre 1839–1842 aus Bonn und Berlin* (Charlottenburg: Egbert Bauer, 1844), 173–77. On the importance of Rotteck's and Welcker's *Staatslexikon* for German

liberalism, see: Sheehan, *German Liberalism*, 84; Lindenfeld, *Practical Imagination*, 110; Woodruff D. Smith, *Politics and the Sciences of Culture in Germany, 1840–1920* (Oxford: Oxford University Press, 1991), 13–34.

38. Karl Marx, "To Dagobert Oppenheim, Approximately August 25, 1842," in *Marx & Engels: Collected Works*, vol. 1 (London: Lawrence & Wishart, 2010), 391–92.

39. Edgar Bauer, "Das Juste-Milieu, Zweiter Artikel," *Rheinische Zeitung für Politik, Handel und Gewerbe* 228 (August 16, 1842): Beiblatt.

40. Edgar Bauer, "Das Juste-Milieu, Zweiter Artikel," *Rheinische Zeitung für Politik, Handel und Gewerbe* 233 (August 21, 1842): Beiblatt.

41. Clark, *Iron Kingdom*, 442–43; Johann Georg August Wirth, *Die Geschichte der deutschen Staaten, Dritter Band* (Karlsruhe: Kunstverlag, 1850), 664–67.

42. Lothar Gall, *Bürgertum in Deutschland* (Berlin: Seidler, 1989), 249; Robert Blum, ed., *Politische Freizüge* (Leipzig: Friese, 1848), 31–42.

43. Edgar Bauer, *Die liberalen Bestrebungen, Erstes Hefte*, 27.

44. Edgar Bauer, *Die liberalen Bestrebungen, Erstes Hefte*, 28.

45. Edgar Bauer, *Die liberalen Bestrebungen, Erstes Hefte*, 33.

46. Edgar Bauer, *Die liberalen Bestrebungen in Deutschland, Zweites Heft. Die Badischen Opposition* (Zurich und Winterthur: Literaischen Comptoirs, 1843), 50.

47. Edgar Bauer, *Die liberalen Bestrebungen, Zweites Heft*, 69.

48. Wirth, *Die Geschichte der deutschen Staaten*, 713; Ernst Dronke, *Berlin* (Frankfurt am Main: Literarische Anstalt, 1846), 242–43.

49. Edgar Bauer, *Georg Herwegh und die literarische Zeitung* (Leipzig: Wigand, 1843), 9, 10.

50. Edgar Bauer, *Georg Herwegh*, 23.

51. Edgar Bauer, *Georg Herwegh*, 25.

52. Edgar Bauer [Anonymous], *Staat, Religion und Parthei* (Leipzig: Wigand, 1843), 4, 5.

53. Edgar Bauer, *Staat, Religion und Parthei*, 18, 19.

54. Edgar Bauer, *Staat, Religion und Parthei*, 20.

55. Wirth, *Die Geschichte der deutschen Staaten*, 718–19; Bauer's own analysis of the new censorship regulations can be found in: Edgar Bauer, *Die Censur-Instruktion vom 31. Januar 1843* (Leipzig: Wigand, 1843). Rather than rejecting the censorship outright, he provides an immanent internal critique, and argues that they cannot accomplish their own stated aims.

56. Herbert De Vriese, "Not a Man of Solid Principles: The Relevance of Edgar Bauer's Polemical Portrait of Karl Marx in His 1843 Novella *Es leben feste Grundsätze!*," *European Journal of the History of Economic Thought* 25, no. 5 (2018): 679–709. See also: Charles Barbour, "'The True Practice Is Theory': Edgar Bauer, Republicanism, and the Young Hegelians," *International Critical Thought* 12, no. 4 (2022): 640–60.

57. Wolfgang Eßbach, *Die Junghegelianer: Soziologie einer Intellektuellengruppe* (Münich: Fink, 1989), 197–202.

58. Edgar Bauer, *Der Streit der Kritik mit Kirche und Staat* (Charlottenburg: Egbert Bauer, 1843), 4, 5.

59. Edgar Bauer, *Der Streit der Kritik*, 5-6.

60. Edgar Bauer, *Der Streit der Kritik*, 9.

61. Edgar Bauer, *Der Streit der Kritik*, 12.

62. Edgar Bauer, *Der Streit der Kritik*, 294.

63. Edgar Bauer, *Der Streit der Kritik*, 296.

64. Edgar Bauer, *Der Streit der Kritik*, 298.

65. Edgar Bauer, *Der Streit der Kritik*, 304.

66. Edgar Bauer, *Der Streit der Kritik*, 305.

67. Edgar Bauer, *Der Streit der Kritik*, 304.

68. Edgar Bauer, *Der Streit der Kritik*, 300.

69. Edgar Bauer, *Der Streit der Kritik*, 310–11.

70. Edgar Bauer, *Der Streit der Kritik*, 314.

71. Edgar Bauer, *Der Streit der Kritik*, 322–23.

72. Edgar Bauer, *Preßproceß Edgar Bauers, über das von ihm verfaßte Werk: Der Streit der Kritik mit Kirche und Staat* (Bern: Jenni, 1844), 79–80.

73. Edgar Bauer, *Preßproceß*, 94–95.

74. Edgar Bauer, *Preßproceß*, 92.

75. Edgar Bauer, *Preßproceß*, 101.

76. Edgar Bauer, *Preßproceß*, 137.

77. The advertisement can be found in: Ernst Jungnitz, *Geschichte des religiösen Lebens in Deutschland* (Charlottenburg: Egbert Bauer, 1844), 215.

78. Bruno Bauer [Anonymous], "Was ist jetzt der Gegenstand der Kritik?," *Allgemeine Literatur-Zeitung: Montasschrift* 8 (July 1844): 20.

79. Edgar Bauer, "Die drei Biedermänner: In drei Capitalen," *Allgemeine Literatur-Zeitung: Monatsschrift* 3 (February 1844): 21.

80. Moses Heß, "Ueber die sozialistische Bewegung in Deutschland," in *Neue Anekdota*, ed. Karl Grün (Darmstadt: Leske, 1845), 188–227; Karl Grün, "Die Bewegung der Produkzion," in *Neue Anekdota*, ed. Karl Grün (Darmstadt: Leske, 1845), 228–46.

81. Karl Marx and Friedrich Engels, *The Holy Family, or Critique of Critical Criticism: Against Bruno Bauer and Company*, in *Marx & Engels: Collected Works*, vol. 4 (London: Lawrence & Wishart, 2010), 23–54.

82. Edgar Bauer [Anonymous], "Proudhon," *Allgemeine Literatur-Zeitung: Monatsschrift* 5 (April 1844): 41.

83. Edgar Bauer [Anonymous], "1842," *Allgemeine Literatur-Zeitung: Monatsschrift* 8 (July 1844): 1.

84. Edgar Bauer, "1842," 6, 7.

85. Edgar Bauer, "1842," 7.

86. See: Bruno Bauer, ed., *Actenstücke zu den Verhandlungen über die Beschlagnahme der Geschichte der Politik, Cultur und Augklärung des achtzenten Jahrhunderts, von Bruno Bauer. Th. 1.* (Christiania: Werner, 1844). Similar to *Preßproceß Edgar Bauers,* this volume provides a record of Bruno Bauer's legal struggle to have the first volume of his history of the eighteenth century published after all copies were confiscated by the police.

87. Martin von Geismar is revealed to be Edgar Bauer in: Julian Schmidt, *Geschichte der deutschen Nationalliteratur im neunzehnten Jahrhundert, Zweiter Band* (Leipzig: Herbig, 1853), 519.

88. Edgar Bauer [Martin von Geismar], "Geschichte des Lutherthums im sechszehnten und siebzehnten Jahrhundert," in *Bibliothek der deutschen Aufklärer der achtzehnten Jahrhunderts, V. Dippel gegen Symbolzwang und Orthodoxie, Edelmann über Dippel, Nebst einer einleitenden Geschichte des Lutherthums im sechszehnten und siebzehnten Jahrhundert,* ed. Edgar Bauer [Martin von Geismar] (Leipzig: Wigand, 1847), 6, 7.

89. Edgar Bauer, "Die Reise auf öffentliche Kosten," *Die Epigonen* 5 (1848): 22.

90. Edgar Bauer, "Die Reise," 27.

91. Edgar Bauer, "Die Reise," 29.

92. Edgar Bauer, "Die Reise," 29, 30.

93. Edgar Bauer, "Die Reise," 112.

94. Schmidt, *Geschichte der deutschen Nationalliteratur,* 432; Stephan Born, *Erinnerungen eines Achtundvierzigers* (Leipzig: Meyer, 1898), 26.

95. Bruno Bauer, *Die bürgerliche Revolution in Deutschland seit dem Anfang der deutsch katholischen Bewegung bis zur Gegenwart* (Berlin: Hempel, 1849).

96. Wilhelm Piersig, *Mysterien der Berliner Demokratie, Erster Theil, Vom März bis zum 12 November 1848* (Berlin: Selbstverlage, 1849), 66–73.

97. Edgar Bauer, *Die Parteien: Politische Revue, Erstes Heft* (Hamburg: Hoffmann und Campe, 1849); Edgar Bauer, *Die Parteien: Politische Revue, Zweites und drittes Heft* (Hamburg: Hoffmann und Campe, 1849).

98. Edgar Bauer, *Die Parteien, Erstes Heft,* 9.

99. Erik Gamby, *Edgar Bauer: Junghegelianer, Publizist, und Polizeiagent, mit Bibliographie der E. Bauer. Texte und Dokumentenanhang* (Trier: Karl-Marx-Haus, 1985); Edgar Bauer, *Konfidentenberichte über die europäische Emigration in London 1852–1861,* ed. Eric Gamby (Trier: Karl-Marx-Haus, 1989),

100.   Eric Gamby, "Einführung," xii–xvii.

101.   Edgar Bauer, *Englische Freiheit* (Leipzig: Wigand, 1857), 22.

102.   Edgar Bauer, *Die Wahrheit über die Internationale* (Altona: Bauer, 1872), 14.

103.   Edgar Bauer, *Das Capital und die Capitalmacht. Grundsätze und Thatsachen zum Verständnis der socialen Frage* (Hannover: Grimm, 1884), 115.

104.   Edgar Bauer, *Capital und die Capitalmacht*, 166.

105.   Edgar Bauer, *Capital und die Capitalmacht*, 172.

106.   Edgar Bauer, *Capital und die Capitalmacht*, 185.

107.   Schmidt, *Geschichte der deutschen Nationalliteratur*, 427–31; "Bauer (Edgar Bauer)," in *Brockhaus' Conversations-Lexikon. Allgemeine deutsche Real Encyklopädie. Zweiter Band* (Leipzig: Brockhaus, 1882), 573.

108.   Max Nettlau, *Geschichte der Anarchie, Band I: Der Vorfrühling der Anarchie* (Berlin: Kater, 1925), 178; Max Nettlau, *A Short History of Anarchism*, trans. Ida Pilat Isca, ed. Heiner M. Becker (London: Freedom Press, 1996), 53.

109.   Gustav Mayer, "Die Anfänge des politischen Radikalismus im vormärzlichen Preußen," *Zeitschrift für Politik* 6 (1913): 5–7, 52–69.

110.   Lawrence Stepelevich, ed., *The Young Hegelians: An Anthology* (Cambridge: Cambridge University Press, 1983), 263–64; Eric V. Luft, "Edgar Bauer and the Origins of the Theory of Terrorism," in *The New Hegelians: Politics and Philosophy in the Hegelian School*, ed. Douglas Moggach (Cambridge: Cambridge University Press, 2006), 136–65; Ingrid Pepperle, *Junghegelianische Geschichtsphilosophie und Kunsttheorie* (Berlin: Akademie-Verlag, 1978), 97.

111.   Eßbach, *Die Junghegelianer*, 202.

112.   Catherine Malabou, *The Future of Hegel: Plasticity, Temporality and Dialectic*, trans. Lisbeth During (Milton Park, UK: Routledge, 2005).

113.   Catherine Malabou, *Stop Thief! Anarchism and Philosophy*, trans. Carolyn Shread (Cambridge, UK: Polity, 2023).

114.   Roberto Esposito, *Institution*, trans. Zakiya Hanafi (Cambridge, UK: Polity, 2022).

115.   Jenny Marx, "Jenny Marx to Engels, About 14 August 1857," in *Marx & Engels: Collected Works*, vol. 40 (London: Lawrence & Wishart, 2010), 565.

116.   Born, *Erinnerungen eines Achtundvierzigers*, 27.

Bibliography

Works by Edgar Bauer

Along with the writings that Edgar Bauer published under his own name, I am including pseudonymous and anonymous texts, as well as edited and coauthored works. I list them in chronological order. This, however, is not intended to be an exhaustive bibliography of Bauer's literary production. It includes only that material explicitly mentioned in this volume.

Bauer, Edgar [E. B.]. "Christoph Columbus. Trauerspiel in 5 Acten. Von K. Werder." *Deutsche Jahrbücher für Wissenschaft und Kunst* 28 (February 3, 1842): 110–12.

Bauer, Edgar. "Vom Geist. Schwert- und Handschlag für Franz Baader. Zur Erwiderung seiner Revision der Philosopheme bezüglich auf das Christenthum. Von Moritz Carriere. Weilburg 1841. Lanz." *Deutsche Jahrbücher für Wissenschaft und Kunst* 37–38 (February 14–15, 1842): 147–52.

Bauer, Edgar. "Monaldeschi oder die Abenteurer. Tragödie in fünf Abtheilungen. von H. Laube." *Deutsche Jahrbücher für Wissenschaft und Kunst* 104 (May 3, 1842): 414–16.

Bauer, Edgar. "Die Bettine als Religionstifterin." *Deutsche Jahrbücher für Wissenschaft und Kunst* 121–22 (May 23-24, 1842): 483–88.

Bauer, Edgar. "Das Juste-Milieu, Erster Artikel." *Rheinische Zeitung für Politik, Handel und Gewerbe* 156 (June 5, 1842).

Bauer, Edgar [Anonymous]. "Fraktionen des Liberalsumus." *Rheinische Zeitung für Politik, Handel und Gewerbe* 170 (June 19, 1842).

Bauer, Edgar [Anonymous]. "Die wahren Liberalen." *Rheinische Zeitung für Politik, Handel und Gewerbe* 171 (June 20, 1842).

Bauer, Edgar [Dr. Radge]. "Die Bruno Bauersche Angelegenheit. Einleitung in die öffentlichen Vorlesungen über die Bedeutung der Hegelschen Philosophie in der christlichen Theologie. Nebst einem Separatvotum über B. Bauer's Kritik der evangelischen Geschichte. Von Dr. Philipp Marheineke. Berlin 1842." *Deutsche Jahrbücher für Wissenschaft und Kunst* 151–54 (June 27–30, 1842): 601–15.

Bauer, Edgar [Dr. Radge]. "Bruno Bauer und die akademische Lehrfreiheit von Dr. O. F. Gruppe. Berlin 1842. Albert Nauck." *Deutsche Jahrbücher für Wissenschaft und Kunst* 173–75 (July 22–25, 1842): 692–98.

Bauer, Edgar [B. Radge]. "Ueber die Anstellung der Theologen an den deutschen Universitäten. Theologisches Votum. Berlin 1842. Berliner Lesecabinet."

Deutsche Jahrbücher für Wissenschaft und Kunst 187–89 (August 8–10, 1842): 745–55.

Bauer, Edgar. "Das Juste-Milieu, Zweiter Artikel." *Rheinische Zeitung für Politik, Handel und Gewerbe* 228, 230, 233, 235 (August 16, 18, 21, 23, 1842.)

Bauer, Edgar [Dr. Radge]. "Protestantische Lehrfreiheit. 1) Minerva, Maiheft 1842. Beitrag zur Verständigung über Begriff und Wesen Nothwendigkeit und Schranken der theologischen Lehrfreiheit. Mit Beziehung auf den Bruno Bauerschen Fall. 2) Bauer und die protestantische Lehrfreiheit, ein politisches Votum." *Deutsche Jahrbücher für Wissenschaft und Kunst* 225–27 (September 21–23, 1842): 897–907.

Bauer, Edgar. *Bruno Bauer und seine Gegner*. Berlin: Jonas, 1842.

Bauer, Edgar [Anonymous]. "Vorläufiges über Bruno Bauer, Kritik der evangelischen Geschichte der Synoptiker." *Deutsche Jahrbücher für Wissenschaft und Kunst* 105 (November 1, 1842): 417–18.

Bauer, Edgar and Friedrich Engels [Anonymous]. *Die frech bedräute, jedoch wunderbar befreite Bibel, oder, Der Triumph des Glaubens*. Neumünster bei Zürich: Heß, 1842.

Bauer, Edgar. "Geschichte Europa's seit der ersten französischen Revolution von Archibald Alison, deutsch von Dr. Ludwig Meyer. Erster und zweiter Band. Leipzig 1842. Otto Wigand." *Deutsche Jahrbücher für Wissenschaft und Kunst* 297–99 (December 14–16, 1842): 1185–95.

Bauer, Edgar. *Die liberalen Bestrebungen in Deutschland, Erstes Heft: Die Ostpreußische Opposition in Deutschland*. Zurich und Winterthur: Literaischen Comptoirs, 1843.

Bauer, Edgar. *Die liberalen Bestrebungen in Deutschland, Zweites Heft: Die Badischen Opposition*. Zurich und Winterthur: Literaischen Comptoirs, 1843.

Bauer, Edgar [Anonymous]. *Georg Herwegh und die literarische Zeitung*. Leipzig: Wigand, 1843.

Bauer, Edgar. *Die Censur-Instruktion vom 31. Januar 1843*. Leipzig: Wigand, 1843.

Bauer, Edgar. "Es leben feste Grundsätze!" In *Berliner Novellen*. Berlin: Berliner Verlags-Buchhandlung, 1843.

Bauer, Edgar [Anonymous]. *Staat, Religion und Parthei*. Leipzig: Wigand, 1843.

Bauer, Edgar. *Der Streit der Kritik mit Kirche und Staat*. Charlottenburg: Egbert Bauer, 1843.

Bauer, Edgar and Bruno Bauer. *Briefwechsel zwischen Bruno Bauer und Edgar Bauer während der Jahre 1839–1842 aus Bonn und Berlin*. Charlottenburg: Egbert Bauer, 1844.

Bauer, Edgar. *Preßproceß Edgar Bauers, über das von ihm verfaßte Werk: Der Streit der Kritik mit Kirche und Staat*. Bern: Jenni, 1844.

Bauer, Edgar. "Die drei Biedermänner: In drei Capitalen." *Allgemeine Literatur-Zeitung: Monatsschrift* 2, nos. 3–5 (February, March, April 1844): 21–28, 38–45, 1–5.

Bauer, Edgar [Anonymous]. "Proudhon." *Allgemeine Literatur-Zeitung: Monatsschrift* 2, no. 5 (April 1844): 37–52.

Bauer, Edgar [Anonymous]. "1842." *Allgemeine Literatur-Zeitung: Monatsschrift* 2, no. 8 (July 1844): 1–8.

Bauer, Edgar. *Die constituirende Versammlung vom October 1789 bis zur Flucht Ludwigs XVI*. Charlottenburg: Egbert Bauer, 1844.

Bauer, Edgar. *Geschichte der constitutionellen und revolutionären Bewegungen im südlichen Deutschland in den Jahren 1831–1834*. Charlottenburg: Egbert Bauer, 1845.

Bauer, Edgar [Martin von Geismar], ed. *Bibliothek der deutschen Aufklärer der achtzehnten Jahrhunderts, I. Carl Friedrich Bahrdt*. Leipzig: Wigand, 1846; *II. Johann August Eberhard's Neue Apologie des Socrates*. Leipzig: Wigand, 1846; *III. Johann Heinrich Schulz*. Leipzig: Wigand, 1846; *IV. Voglers Superintendenten zu Bayreuth Evangelist Johannes vor dem jüngsten* Gericht. Leipzig: Wigand, 1846; *V. Dippel gegen Symbolzwang und Orthodoxie Edelmann über Dippel, Nebst einer einleitenden Geschichte des Lutherthums im sechszehnten und siebzehnten Jahrhundert*. Leipzig: Wigand, 1847.

Bauer, Edgar [Martin von Geismar], ed. *Die politische Literatur der Deutschen im achtzehnten Jahrhundert, I. Politische Aufklärer aus der Zeit der Französischen Revolution*. Leipzig: Wigand, 1847; *II. Politische Märtyrer aus der Zeit der französischen Revolution*. Leipzig: Wigand, 1847; *III. Deutsche Zustände in den siebziger und achtziger Jahren des vorigen Jahrhunderts und der Feldzug in die Champagne nach den Schilderungen eines* sujet perdu. Leipzig: Wigand, 1847; *IV. Erfahrungen und Bemerkungen eines preußischen Emissärs in der französischen Republik währen der Jahre 1793-1795*. Leipzig: Wigand, 1847.

Bauer, Edgar. "Die Reise auf öffentliche Kosten," *Die Epigonen* 5 (1848): 9–122.

Bauer, Edgar. *Die Parteien. Politische Revue. Erstes Heft*. Hamburg: Hoffmann und Campe, 1849.

Bauer, Edgar. *Die Parteien. Politische Revue. Zweites und drittes Heft*. Hamburg: Hoffmann und Campe, 1849.

Bauer, Edgar. *Englische Freiheit*. Leipzig: Wigand, 1857.

Bauer, Edgar [Anonymous]. *Reflections on the Integrity of the Danish Monarchy*. London: Wertheim and Macintosh, 1857.

Bauer, Edgar [Anonymous]. *Schleiswig*. London: Wertheim, Macintosh and Hunt, 1861.

Bauer, Edgar [Anonymous]. *Eine Denkschrift für die holsteinische Stände-Versammlung. Von* einem Preußen. Berlin: Heinicke, 1863.

Bauer, Edgar. *Das teutsche Reich in seiner geschichtlichen: Gestalt zugleich ein Beitrag zur Prüfung des Ursprungs der Teutschen, Gerusker, Kelten und Slaven.* Altona: Bauer, 1872.

Bauer, Edgar. *Die Wahrheit über die Internationale.* Altona: Bauer, 1872.

Bauer, Edgar. *Artikel V, der deutsche Gedanke und die dänische Monarchie.* Altona: Bauer, 1873.

Bauer, Edgar. *Der Freimaurerbund und das Licht. Bausteine zur Geschichte der Loge und der religiösen Sage.* Hannover: Bauer, 1877.

Bauer, Edgar. *Zwei Ordensskizzen: I Die Independent Odd-Fellows Englands und Amerikas. II Gotthold Ephraim Lessing als Ordensbruder.* Leipzig: Grimm, 1881.

Bauer, Edgar. *Der Magnus des Nordens, Novella.* Leipzig: Grimm, 1882.

Bauer, Edgar. *Das Capital und die Capitalmacht. Grundsätze und Thatsachen zum Verständnis der socialen Frage.* Hannover: Grimm, 1884.

Bauer, Edgar. *Konfidentenberichte über die europäische Emigration in London 1852–1861.* edited by Eric Gamby. Trier: Karl-Marx-Haus, 1989.

Other Works Cited

Alison, Archibald. *History of Europe from the Commencement of the French Revolution in 1789 to the Restoration of the Bourbons in 1815. In Four Volumes.* New York: Harper, 1842.

Anonymous. "Bauer (Edgar Bauer)." In *Brockhaus' Conversations-Lexikon. Allgemeine deutsche Real Encyklopädie. Zweiter Band.* Leipzig: Brockhaus, 1882.

Anonymous. "Literarisches Forum. Berliner Novellen. Von A. Weill und Edgar Bauer. Berlin, Berliner Verlagshandlung. 1843." In *Berliner Wespen. Fünftes Heft.* Edited by Feodor Wehl, 42–44. Leipzig: Recalm, 1843.

Anonymous, "Novellen. 1. Berliner Novellen. Von A. Weill und Edgar Bauer. Berliner Verlagsbuchhandlung. 1843." *Literaturblatt* 115 (November 10, 1843): 460.

Anonymous. "Preußen seit der Einfeßung Arndt's bis zur Abfeßung Bauers." In *Einundzwanzig Bogen aus der Schweiz.* Edited by Georg Herwegh, 1–31. Zürich und Winterthur: Literarischen Comptoirs, 1843.

Anonymous, "Unterhaltungsliteratur. 1. Berliner Novellen. Von A. Weill und Edgar Bauer. Berlin, Berliner Verlagsbuchhandlung. 1843." *Blätter für literarische Unterhaltung* 146 (May 25, 1844): 583.

Barbour, Charles. "A Liberal Before Liberalism: Karl Hermann Scheidler and the New Hegelians." *Modern Intellectual History* 18 (2021): 658–80.

Barbour, Charles. "Partisan of the Absolute State: Arnold Ruge, Liberalism, and the *Hallische Jahrbücher.*" *Central European History* (first view).

Barbour, Charles. "The Political Theology and Polemical Tactics of Bruno Bauer." *The European Legacy* 29, no. 2 (2024): 143–65.

Barbour, Charles. "'The True Practice Is Theory': Edgar Bauer, Republicanism, and the Young Hegelians." *International Critical Thought* 12, no. 4 (2022): 640–60.

Bauer, Bruno ed. *Actenstücke zu den Verhandlungen über die Beschlagnahme der Geschichte der Politik, Cultur und Augklärung des achtzenten Jahrhunderts, von Bruno Bauer. Th. 1.* Christiania: Werner, 1844.

Bauer, Bruno. "Das Leben Jesu, kritisch bearbeiten, Erster Band." *Jahrbücher für wissenschaftliche Kritik* 109–13 (1837): 879–912.

Bauer, Bruno. "Das Leben Jesu, kritisch bearbeiten, Zweiter Band." *Jahrbücher für wissenschaftliche Kritik* 86–88 (1836): 681–704.

Bauer, Bruno. *Die bürgerliche Revolution in Deutschland seit dem Anfang der deutsch katholischen Bewegung bis zur Gegenwart.* Berlin: Hempel, 1849.

Bauer, Bruno. *Die evangelische Landeskirche Preussens und die Wissenschaft.* Leipzig: Wigand, 1840.

Bauer, Bruno. *Die gute Sache der Frieheit und meine eigene Angelegenheit.* Zürich und Winterthur: Literarischen Comptoirs, 1842.

Bauer, Bruno. *Herr Dr. Hengstenberg. Kritische Briefe über den Gegensaß des Geseßes und des Evangelium.* Berlin: Dümmler, 1839.

Bauer, Bruno. *Kritik der evangelischen Geschichte der Synoptiker, Erster Band.* Leipzig: Wigand, 1842.

Bauer, Bruno. *Kritik der Geschichte der Offenbarung. Die Religion Des Alten Testamentes in der geschichtlichen Entwickelung ihrer Principien dargestellt, Erster Band.* Berlin: Dümmler, 1838.

Bauer, Bruno. "Schriften über Strauss Leben Jesu." *Jahrbücher für wissenschaftliche Kritik* 41–43 (1837): 321–40.

Bauer, Bruno [Anonymous]. "Was ist jetzt der Gegenstand der Kritik?" *Allgemeine Literatur-Zeitung: Montasschrift* 8 (July 1844): 18-26.

Biedermann, Karl. *Die deutsche Philosophie vom Kant bis unsre Zeit, Zweiter Band.* Leipzig: Meyer und Wigand, 1842.

Bigler, Robert M. *The Politics of German Protestantism.* Berkeley: University of California Press, 1972.

Blum, Robert, ed. *Politische Freizüge.* Leipzig: Friese, 1848.

Born, Stephan. *Erinnerungen eines Achtundvierzigers.* Leipzig: Meyer, 1898.

Breckman, Warren. *Marx, the Young Hegelians, and the Origins of Radical Social Theory: Dethroning the Self.* Cambridge: Cambridge University Press, 1999.

Clark, Christopher. "Confessional Policy and the Limits of State Action: Frederick William III and the Prussian Church Union 1817–40." *Historical Journal* 39, no. 4 (December 1996): 985–1004.

Clark, Christopher. "Germany 1815–1848: Restoration or Pre-March?" In *Nineteenth-Century Germany: Politics, Culture and Society, 1780–1918*. Edited by John Breuilly, 27–48. London: Bloomsbury, 2001.

Clark, Christopher. *Iron Kingdom: The Rise and Downfall of Prussia, 1600–1947*. Cambridge: Belknap Press, 2006.

Clark, Christopher. "Religion." In *Germany 1800–1870*. Edited by Jonathan Sperber, 162–84. Oxford: Oxford University Press, 2004.

De Vriese, Herbert. "Not a Man of Solid Principles: The Relevance of Edgar Bauer's Polemical Portrait of Karl Marx in His 1843 Novella *Es leben feste Grundsätze!*" *European Journal of the History of Economic Thought* 25, no. 5 (2018): 679–709.

Dronke, Ernst. *Berlin, Erster Band*. Frankfurt am Main: Literarische Anstalt, 1846.

Dronke, Ernst. *Berlin, Zweiter Band*. Frankfurt am Main: Literarische Anstalt, 1846.

Eßbach, Wolfgang. *Die Junghegelianer: Soziologie einer Intellektuellengruppe*. Münich: Fink, 1989.

Esposito, Roberto. *Institution*. Translated by Zakiya Hanafi. Cambridge, UK: Polity, 2022.

Evangelisch-theologischen Facultät der Rheinischen Friedrich-Wilhelms-Universität. *Gutachten der Evangelisch theologischen Facultäten der Königlich Preußischen Universitäten über den Licentiaten Bruno Bauer in Beziehung auf dessen Kritik der evangelischen Geschichte der Synoptiker*. Berlin: Dümmler, 1842.

Gall, Lothar. *Bürgertum in Deutschland*. Berlin: Seidler, 1989.

Gamby, Eric. *Edgar Bauer: Junghegelianer, Publizist, und Polizeiagent, mit Bibliographie der E. Bauer. Texte und Dokumentenanhang*. Trier: Karl-Marx-Haus, 1985.

Gamby, Eric. "Einführung." In *Konfidentenberichte über die europäische Emigration in London 1852–1861*. Edited by Eric Gamby, xi–xviii. Trier: Karl-Marx-Haus, 1989.

Grün, Karl. "Die Bewegung der Produkzion." In *Neue Anekdota*. Edited by Karl Grün, 228–46. Darmstadt: Leske, 1845.

Gruppe, Otto Friedrich. *Bruno Bauer und die akademische Lehrfreiheit*, Berlin: Rauck, 1842.

Heine, Heinrich. *The Poems of Heinrich Heine*. Translated by Edgar Bauer Alfred Bowring. London: Bell and Daldy, 1866.

Hengstenberg, Ernst. "Die Vollbrachte Revolution." *Evangelische Kirchenzeitung* 57 (1842): 449–51.

Heß, Moses. "Ueber die sozialistische Bewegung in Deutschland." In *Neue Anekdota*. Edited by Karl Grün, 1882–77. Darmstadt: Leske, 1845.

Hohendahl, Peter Uwe. "Literary Criticism in the Epoch of Liberalism, 1820–70." In *A History of German Literary Criticism, 1780–1980*. Edited by Peter Uwe Hohendahl, 179–276. Lincoln: University of Nebraska Press.

Hook, Sidney. *From Hegel to Marx: Studies in the Intellectual Development of Karl Marx*. New York: John Day, 1936.

Jacoby, Johann [Anonymous]. *Vier Fragen, beantwortet von einem Ostpreußen*. Mannheim: Hoff, 1841.

Jungnitz, Ernst. *Geschichte des religiösen Lebens in Deutschland*. Charlottenburg: Egbert Bauer, 1844.

Lambrecht, Lars ed. *"Umstürzende Gedanken": Radikale Theorie im Vorfeld der 1848er Revolution*. Frankfurt am Main: Peter Lang, 2013.

Leipold, Bruno. *Citizen Marx: Republicanism and the Formation of Karl Marx's Social and Political Thought*. Princeton: Princeton University Press, 2024.

Leonhard, Jörn. "Formulating and Reformulating 'Liberalism.'" In *In Search of European Liberalisms: Concepts, Languages, Ideologies*. Edited by Fernández-Sebastián Freeden and Jörn Leonhard, 72–101. Oxford: Oxford University Press, 2019.

Lindenfeld, David F. *The Practical Imagination: The German Sciences of State in the Nineteenth Century*. Chicago: University of Chicago Press, 1997.

Luft, Eric V. "Edgar Bauer and the Origins of the Theory of Terrorism." In *The New Hegelians: Politics and Philosophy in the Hegelian School*. Edited by Douglas Moggach, 136–65. Cambridge: Cambridge University Press, 2006.

Mah, Harold. *The End of Philosophy and the Origin of Ideology: Karl Marx and the Crisis of the Young Hegelians*. Berkeley: University of California Press, 1987.

Malabou, Catherine. *The Future of Hegel: Plasticity, Temporality and Dialectic*. Translated by Lisbeth During. Milton Park, UK: Routledge, 2005.

Malabou, Catherine. *Stop Thief! Anarchism and Philosophy*. Translated by Carolyn Shread. Cambridge, UK: Polity, 2023.

Marheineke, Philipp Konrad. *Einleitung in die öffentlichen Vorlesungen über die Bedeutung der Hegelschen Philosophie in der christlichen Theologie, Nebst einem Separatvotum über B. Bauers Kritik der evangelischen Geschichte*. Berlin: Enslin, 1842.

Marx, Jenny. "Jenny Marx to Engels, About 14 August 1857." In *Marx & Engels: Collected Works*. Vol. 40, 565. London: Lawrence & Wishart, 2010.

Marx, Karl. *The Civil War in France*. In *Marx & Engels: Collected Works*. Vol. 22, 307–59. London: Lawrence & Wishart, 2010.

Marx, Karl. *The Poverty of Philosophy: Answer to the Philosophy of Poverty by M. Proudhon*. In *Marx & Engels: Collected Works*. Vol. 6, 105–212. London: Lawrence & Wishart, 2010.

Marx, Karl. "To Dagobert Oppenheim, Approximately August 25, 1842." In *Marx & Engels: Collected Works*. Vol. 1, 391–92. London: Lawrence & Wishart, 2010.

Marx, Karl, and Friedrich Engels. *The German Ideology*. In *Marx & Engels: Collected Works*. Vol. 4. London: Lawrence & Wishart, 2010.

Marx, Karl, and Friedrich Engels. *The Holy Family, or Critique of Critical Criticism*. In *Marx & Engels: Collected Works*. Vol. 4. London: Lawrence & Wishart, 2010.

Mayer, Gustav. "Die Anfänge des politischen Radikalismus im vormärzlichen Preußen." *Zeitschrift für Politik* 6 (1913): 1–113.

McLellan, David. *The Young Hegelians and Karl Marx*. London: Praeger, 1969.

Moggach, Douglas, ed. *The New Hegelians: Philosophy and Politics in the Hegelian School*. Cambridge: Cambridge University Press, 2006.

Moggach, Douglas. *The Philosophy and Politics of Bruno Bauer*. Cambridge: Cambridge University Press, 2003.

Mommsen, Wolfgang J. "German Liberalism in the Nineteenth Century." In *The Cambridge History of Nineteenth-Century Political Thought*. Edited by Gareth Stedman Jones and Gregory Claeys, 409–32. Cambridge: Cambridge University Press, 2011.

Nettlau, Max. *Geschichte der Anarchie, Band I: Der Vorfrühling der Anarchie*. Berlin: Kater, 1925.

Nettlau, Max. *A Short History of Anarchism*. Translated by Ida Pilat Isca, edited by Heiner M. Becker. London: Freedom Press, 1996.

Pepperle, Ingrid. *Junghegelianische Geschichtsphilosophie und Kunsttheorie*. Berlin: Akademie-Verlag, 1978.

Piersig, Wilhelm. *Mysterien der Berliner Demokratie, Erster Theil, Vom März bis zum 12 November 1848*. Berlin: Selbstverlage, 1849.

Proudhon, Pierre Joseph. *Qu'est-ce que la propriété? ou, Recherches sur le principe du Gouvernement*. Paris: Prévot, 1841.

Proudhon, Pierre Joseph. *Système des contradictions économiques, ou, Philosophie de la misère*. Paris: Guillaumin, 1846.

Pruß, Robert. *Vorlesungen über die deutsche Literatur der Gegenwart*. Leipzig: Mayer, 1847.

Pruß, Robert. *Zehn Jahre. Geschichte der neuesten Zeit. 1840–1850. Zweiter Band*. Leipzig: Weber, 1856.

Quante, Michael, and Amir Mohseni, eds. *Die linken Hegelianer: Studien zum Verhältnis von Religion und Politik im Vormärz*. Leiden: Brill, 2015.

Ruge, Arnold. "Die Hegelsche Rechtsphilosophie und die Politik unserer Zeit." *Deutsche Jahrbücher für Wissenschaft und Kunst* 189–92 (August 10–13, 1842): 755–68.

Ruge, Arnold. "Zur Kritik des gegenwartigen Staats- und Völkerrechts." *Hallische Jahrbücher für deutsche Wissenschaft und Kunst* 151–56 (June 24–30, 1840): 1201–43.

Sass, Friedrich. *Berlin in seiner neuesten Zeit und Entwicklung.* Leipzig: Koffka, 1846.

Scheidler, Karl Hermann [Anonymous]. "Beitrag zur Verständigung über Begriff und Wesen, Nothwendigkeit und Schranken der theologischen Lehrfreiheit (mit Beziehung auf dern Bruno Bauer'schen Fall)." In *Minerva, Zweiter Band.* Edited by Friedrich Bran, 321–59. Jena: Bran, 1842.

Scheidler, Karl Hermann. "Hegel (Neuhegelianer)." In *Das Staats-Lexikon, Sechster Band.* Edited by Carl Rotteck and Carl Welcker. Altona: Hammerich, 1847.

Schmidt, Julian. *Geschichte der deutschen Literatur im neunzehnten Jahrhundert. Dritter Band. Die Gegenwart.* Leipzig: Herbig, 1855.

Schmidt, Julian. *Geschichte der deutschen Nationalliteratur im neunzehnten Jahrhundert, Zweiter Band.* Leipzig: Herbig, 1853.

Seigel, Jerrold. "European Liberalism in the Nineteenth Century." In *The Cambridge History of Modern European Thought.* Edited by Warren Breckman and Peter E. Gordon, 172–95. Cambridge: Cambridge University Press, 2019.

Sheehan, James J. *German Liberalism in the Nineteenth Century.* Chicago: University of Chicago Press, 1978.

Skinner, Quentin. *Visions of Politics.* Vol. 1, *Regarding Method.* Cambridge: Cambridge University Press, 2002.

Smith, Woodruff D. *Politics and the Sciences of Culture in Germany, 1840–1920.* Oxford: Oxford University Press, 1991.

Stedman Jones, Gareth. "The Young Hegelians, Marx and Engels." In *The Cambridge History of Nineteenth-Century Political Thought.* Edited by Gareth Stedman Jones and Gregory Claeys, 556–600. Cambridge: Cambridge University Press, 2011.

Stepelevich, Lawrence, ed. *The Young Hegelians: An Anthology.* Cambridge: Cambridge University Press, 1983.

Stolleis, Michael. *Public Law in Germany: A Historical Introduction from the 16th to the 21st Century.* Translated by Thomas Dunlap. Oxford: Oxford University Press, 2017.

Strauss, David Friedrich. *Das Leben Jesu kritisch bearbeitet. Erster Band.* Tübingen: Osiander, 1835.

Strauss, David Friedrich. *Das Leben Jesu kritisch bearbeitet. Zweiter Band.* Tübingen: Osiander, 1836.

Strauss, David Friedrich. *Streitschriften zur vertheidigung meiner schrift über das Leben Jesu, Drittes Heft.* Tübingen: Osiender, 1837.

Toews, John E. "Church and State." In *The Cambridge History of Nineteenth-Century Political Thought*. Edited by Gareth Stedman Jones and Gregory Claeys, 603–48. Cambridge: Cambridge University Press, 2011.

Vizetelly, Henry. *Berlin Under the New Empire*. Vol. 1. London: Tinsley Brothers, 1879.

Wirth, Johann Georg August. *Die Geschichte der deutschen Staaten, Dritter Band*. Karlsruhe: Kunstverlag, 1850.

Index of Names